Grades **2-3**

Linda Hoyt and Teresa Therriault

Mastering *the* Mechanics

Ready-to-Use Lessons for Modeled, Guided, and Independent Editing

NEW YORK • TORONTO • LONDON • AUCKLAND • SYDNEY
MEXICO CITY • NEW DELHI • HONG KONG • BUENOS AIRES

Credits
Ruth Culham's Copy Editor's Symbols
Rebecca Sitton's High-Frequency Writing Words

Cover design by Jay Namerow
Interior design by Maria Lilja
Interior photos by Linda Hoyt, Teresa Therriault, and Patrick Burke
Acquiring editor: Lois Bridges
Production editor: Erin K.L. Grelak
Copy Editor: David Klein

ISBN 13: 978-0-545-04878-1
ISBN 10: 0-545-04878-8

3 4 5 6 7 8 9 10   23   12 11 10 09

We dedicate this to our husbands, Steve and Darrel. They make us smile, support us in countless ways, and love to remind us how lucky we are to have their love and support. They are right. We are wonderfully lucky to have them. Thanks, guys!

ACKNOWLEDGMENTS

We feel fortunate to have worked together for many years as Title I teachers, staff developers, and friends. Through these years, we have had many mentors along the way who have helped us lift our practice, challenge our thinking, and find the courage to reach beyond what we knew yesterday. Those mentors include our colleagues, the children we have had the honor to serve, and those powerful professionals whose books on writing constantly challenge and inform us. Donald Graves, Donald Murray, Shelley Harwayne, Lucy Calkins, Regie Routman, Ralph Fletcher, Katie Wood Ray, and many others have carried the torch and helped us all make a bigger difference for young writers.

At Kinnaman Elementary in Beaverton, Oregon, Jan McCall, principal, opened her heart and the classrooms of her wonderful learning community so that we could capture the photos that appear in this resource and on the cover. Their beautiful children, led by Marie Davis, Melissa Suesserman, Angie Thomas, Heidi Cochran, Traci Orth, and Patty Jo Foley, stretched our thinking and confirmed the validity of these cycles.

The lessons in this resource were carefully tested to ensure they were classroom-ready and reflective of the challenges young editors face. Piloting educators included district administrators, teachers, principals, and consultants. Their feedback to the learning cycles put muscle behind our thinking through their insightful observations of learners and helpful suggestions. In Davidson County, North Carolina, our heartfelt thanks go to Sonja Parks, April Willard, Wendy Younts, Leigh Ann Bruff, Amber Idol, Amber Parker, Stephanie Ward, Tricia Prevette, and Emily Lipe. In Ukiah, California, we thank Kathryn McInnis, Debbee Freeman, Cathy Hessom, Gayle Kline, Janet McLeod, Caryl Mastrof, and Leslie Maricle-Barclay for opening their thinking and their classrooms to engage with the lessons. Kelly Boswell and Barbara Coleman, master teachers and independent consultants, provided valuable affirmations and encouragement.

We have found it quite joyous to get to know the team at Scholastic. Lois Bridges, our amazing editor and trusted friend, is a cherished anchor, always smoothing the way with careful suggestions, time-saving support, and unflagging optimism. Eagle-eye "Grammar Goddess" Gloria Pipkin is our indispensable safety net. Terry Cooper, Ray Coutu, David Klein, Maria Lilja, and Erin K. L. Grelak have generously shared their thinking, expanded our vision, and helped this resource take shape in the teacher-friendly manner we so wished to achieve. It has been a pleasure, and we thank them sincerely.

TABLE OF CONTENTS

To print out the reproducibles at full size in the Tools, Assessment and Record Keeping, and Appendix: Student Writing Samples sections, please visit www.scholastic.com/masteringthemechanics.

PART I

Introduction: Mastering the Mechanics

Putting Editing in Perspective

We care about the conventions of written language and we are not alone. The parents of the children we serve, the community, and the public all care about and expect children to show growing expertise in the conventions of written language: to present written work in such a way that it is legible, spelled correctly, and demonstrates correct grammar, capitalization, and punctuation.

As we focus young learners on mechanics and conventions, we want to be very clear about our goals:

1. To nurture writers who understand that rich, well-crafted messages are their first and most important focus.

2. To help children understand that a study of mechanics and conventions is about adding tools that enhance our messages, not just about correcting and being "right."

It is important to state that we are not in favor of prepackaged programs that cast editing and conventions as "mistakes" or exercises in correction. These programs have very little embedded instruction and consistently overwhelm students with sentences that are so laden with errors that meaning is easily lost, leaving a writer with few connections to his or her own work.

> **"** Just as the baker who creates a cake from scratch takes pride in adding butter-cream roses atop chocolate swirls, students must learn to delight in knowing how to add the important touches of correct spelling, grammar, and punctuation. **"**
> —*Shelley Harwayne*

conventions
(spacing, handwriting, spelling, and grammar)

mechanics
(periods, capital letters, and so on)

Above all, as we cast our attention upon mechanics and conventions we must be sure that creative thinking flourishes during drafting and revision. If mechanics and editing are overemphasized, they can have the negative effect of reducing writing volume, by causing children to limit their writing to words they are able to spell correctly or to use overly simplistic sentence structures.

Recast Mechanics and Conventions as Tools to Lift Writing Quality

Writers must understand that mechanics are not tedious obligations. They are tools that add clarity and interest to our writing. Carefully conceived modeled writing lessons improve craft, mechanics, grammar, and spelling. Our goal is to develop the understanding that writers integrate conventions into craft rather than seeing them simply as elements of "correctness." Modeled writing with a think-aloud recasting mechanics as craft might sound like this:

> I want to write about how quiet it was when I was walking in the woods.
> I could say: "I went walking in the woods. It was quiet." That is okay, but if I think about how punctuation can help me write in more interesting ways, I think I can make it even better.
>
> What do you think of: "Shhh! Listen! As my feet crunch softly on the gravel path, the sound seems huge. It is so quiet in the forest that my footsteps sound loud!" Look how I used exclamation marks. They helped my opening and my ending to be more interesting. And do you see the comma I used? That told my reader to take a little breath so the ending of my sentence is more dramatic. Using punctuation makes my writing better!

It is our sincere hope that this resource will help educators and children alike see conventions and mechanics through new eyes. We believe conventions and mechanics are naturally woven into the writing process at two major points.

1. During drafting: Conventions and mechanics support our messages and enhance communication. Carefully chosen punctuation can clarify, control volume and flow, plus make ideas sparkle!

2. During editing: Conventions and mechanics provide readers with access to our thinking. Correct spelling, grammar, spacing, and punctuation make our work accessible to readers.

Steep Conventions in Meaning

We believe that we must keep the focus on meaning while steeping learners in conventions and mechanics. With this emphasis, it would be perfectly natural to have a modeled writing that looks and sounds something like this:

> I love popcorn. I love the crackly crunch and poppety pop as kernels start to explode. One of the things I love is that the "pop" sometimes surprises me. I am going to use exclamation marks to show that in my writing. Watch to see how I use exclamation marks to make my meaning more clear. I add the exclamation mark {!} so the reader knows it was a quick burst of sound.

> "Pop! Pop! Poppety! I can hardly wait for those salty, crunchy bits to land on my tongue."

By recasting punctuation as a tool that can make our writing sparkle, we have maintained a clear focus on meaning. This kind of work on mechanics and conventions enriches communication and elevates writing quality.

Tiptoe Lightly With "Correctness"

We must avoid a situation where the fear of being incorrect freezes writers and forces them into a narrow zone of "correctness." In this kind of setting, writers can sometimes place too much emphasis on spelling, for example, and begin to limit their writing to words they know they can spell correctly. This dangerously limits the writing within the confines of spelling rather than letting it flourish through the writer's sense of language and imagination. While empowering writers with conventions, we must also take seriously our mission to keep meaning as the primary objective. Our goal: Language is lifted and elaborated with mechanics as a subset of the message.

> Conventions and mechanics should support meaning, not limit it.

Have High Expectations

We do believe, however, that it is appropriate to set expectations and to make it clear to children that after completing a cycle, they have new tools they can use and are expected to use. After a lesson on capitalizing names and places, it is perfectly reasonable to expect writers to apply that convention in their writing. After a lesson on rereading to check for sentence fragments, it is reasonable to expect writers to reread for the same purpose. As we tread lightly with conventions, we can still have high expectations for our students' development and growth.

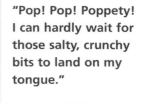

> ❚❚The last thing you want is for your children to settle for 'The dog bit at me,' instead of writing 'The dog snarled at me,' because of a concern for correctness. ❚❚
> —*Lucy Calkins and Natalie Louis*

Rereading Power

- What do I see?
- Is the writing neat enough for someone else to read?
- Do my picture and my words make good use of space on the page?
- Does my punctuation add to the message?
- Did I use a capital letter to start my sentences?
- How is the spelling?
- What words should I revisit?
- Have I used what I know about strong openers and commas to draw in my reader?

Rereading: A Strategic Tool for Meaning, Mechanics, and Conventions

- Rereading during *drafting* helps our ideas flow and helps us regain momentum with the message we are crafting.

- Rereading during *revision* helps us wonder about craft elements such as word choice, interesting leads, voice, volume, and focus of information. It is also a time when we can wonder if our punctuation is used in ways that help the reader, add clarity to our thinking, and make the writing more interesting.

- Rereading when we *edit for an audience* takes on an entirely different dimension. This is the time when we slow down and really look at the visual dimensions of what we have created.

Rereading: Focused Edits

When students reread to edit for conventions and mechanics, we believe it is most effective if you have them engage in focused edits. In a focused edit, the writer reads with a focus on a single purpose. For example, the writer might reread once to check for end punctuation. Then, the writer rereads again to check for capital letters. Each editing point gets its own rereading. Focused edits with a single purpose for each rereading help writers target their editing purpose.

First focused edit: Reread for capital letters.

Second focused edit: Reread *through a new lens* to check for end punctuation.

When writers reread for all editing elements at the same time, they can be overwhelmed and overlook points they are capable of lifting to a conventional level.

" Writers take their reading very seriously. When they read, they discover topics for their own writing. They become interested in new genres and formats. They study authors' techniques to learn how to improve their own writing. **"**
    —Shelley Harwayne

Focus on Reading and Writing as Reciprocal Processes

Reading and writing are reciprocal language processes. As writers create text, they are constantly rereading their work and applying all they know about how print works. When writers read, they are seeing models of language, spacing, conventional spelling, and punctuation that will inform their work as writers (Calkins & Louis, 2003). Reading and writing are powerful partners, each extending and transforming the network of literacy understandings being constructed within our students. Research suggests that in classrooms where children write about their reading, embrace mentor texts as writing tutors, and consider writing a natural link to reading, academic achievement is lifted (Taylor, Pearson, Peterson, & Rodriguez, 2005; Graves, 1994). The key is to make the reciprocal relationship between reading and writing transparent to our students as we immerse them in intensive and extensive experiences with print.

Highlight Mechanics and Conventions in Mentor Texts

We have become accustomed to turning to wonderful mentor texts to enrich children's exposure to literary language, form, and craft. It is helpful to consider that

Reread familiar favorites to count question marks and periods.

Compare the use of question marks across favorite selections.

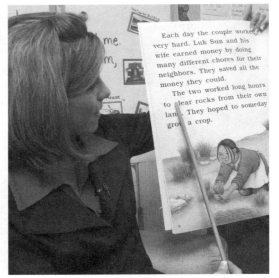

Shared reading is a perfect time to highlight the ways in which authors use conventions.

Just then, a lazy goose came by and laid an egg in Mother Duck's nest.

The goose hid the egg under some leaves.

Notice how the comma makes the opener, "just then," stand out and draw the attention of the reader. (Reprinted from *What a Duck*, Rigby, Literacy by Design, 2008)

❝ I often think that when I watch a really good teacher of writing, it's almost like there are life-size cardboard cutouts of authors all around the room. Jane Yolen is standing up by the chalkboard and Eloise Greenfield is just by the door to welcome students as they enter.... With a room full of authors to help us, teaching writing... and reading... doesn't have to be so lonely. **❝**
—*Katie Wood Ray*

children's literature is also one of our most powerful tools for celebrating and noticing the interesting ways in which writers use spacing, punctuation, capitalization, and grammar. Encouraging children to reread and look closely at a familiar text helps them attend to the fine points, noticing the frequency of end punctuation marks, spacing, or purposes for capital letters. Presenting mechanics within literature provides a tapestry of opportunity in which to explore mechanics, while helping children to understand that *all writers* think about spacing, grammar, punctuation, spelling, and so on.

Modeling: The Heart of Our Work

We believe it is critical to do a great deal of modeled writing as the children observe and listen to us think out loud about conventions and mechanics and how they are woven into our messages. We *show* writers how we use letters, sounds, punctuation, and grammar to make our thinking accessible to a reader. We believe that every day children should have the chance to observe the creation of quality writing that has artistic punctuation, and jaw-dropping phrasing, and sets a model that they can attempt to emulate.

Explicit demonstrations of writing are central to the work we do as writing coaches. When we model interesting openings, insertion of onomatopoeia with an exclamation mark, or show how to write items in a list, we are clarifying our students' vision of quality writing.

Modeled writing, like the picture on the front of a jigsaw puzzle box, sets the stage and helps writers establish a vision of possibility for their work as writers. It is a forum for sharing a broad range of genre, interesting sentence formations, sizzling interjections, and mood-altering phrasing. It is the springboard from which quality student writing evolves. Like read-alouds, modeled writing should be crafted by you as an expert, showing the best of what can be. This is when we show, rather than tell, what great writing looks like and sounds like. This is *not* a time to write like a child, but rather a time to open the door

Never ask students to do something they haven't watched you do first.

Important Note: Save your modeled writings! Students like to refer back to them, and you can use them for think-alouds on editing and revising.

into the world of wonderful possibility that awaits as writers gain control over their craft. Write at the top of your own game. Pull out all the stops with word choice, phrasing, and interesting punctuation. You will be amazed at how quickly elements of your quality work will begin to appear in the writing of your students.

Think Out Loud During Modeled Writing

The think-alouds we provide during modeled writing make the inner workings of the writing process transparent to children. If we allow our talk to flow around the creation of printed text, children can listen in as we make decisions about word choice, spelling, punctuation, and grammar. Let them ride with you on your writing journey as you construct and deconstruct your thinking. Talk about what you hope to say, let them hear you think as you make choices, celebrate in front of your students when you think of a fascinating way to use punctuation to power up your writing. There is no more powerful lesson for your students than watching as you think out loud about phrasing or word choice, pause midstream to reread and see how everything is coming together, and then return to drafting.

> During a modeled write, the focus is on cracking open the writing process so the internal thinking of an experienced writer becomes transparent to the students.

Think-alouds during modeled writing open the door to the wonders that occur as we think, write, reread, then write again. Think-alouds show learners how we massage messages, selecting the words and the conventions that make our ideas come alive on paper.

Model Rereading and Marking Up a Text

As we model drafting, revising, and editing, we need to help students understand that these essential processes can be messy work. Young writers need to observe us changing our mind, crossing out words or even entire lines. They need to see how we might read a line, stand back, and say something like:

> I just wrote, "The dog barked." That is okay but it sure isn't very interesting. I am going to scratch that out and write this sentence another way. This is a good time to use what I know about <u>sentence openers and commas</u> to make the sentence

sparkle. What do you think of, "With a low rumble that started deep in his chest, the dog's bark erupted into a storm of moving fur."

A rewrite like this isn't tidy, but is it good for writers? You bet! Show your students how to actively wrestle with the creation of clear, sparkling messages that are empowered by punctuation and strong visual images. Show them how to scratch over, scratch out, and get a bit messy as they draft. Help them understand that this is what writers do during drafting, revising, and again during editing when they are looking to fine-tune spelling, spacing, punctuation, and so forth. A well marked–up page often suggests that the writer/editor is thinking deeply.

Joys of Developing Writing

Writing in second and third grade is exciting. Students at this age have a sense of fluency and purpose as they pick up their writing tools. They are gaining control over a range of text forms, such as personal narrative, procedural texts, descriptive reports, and personal letters. At this stage of writing development, we can expect that most will be using basic sentence structures and will show some variation in sentence beginnings.

Because developing writers have these skills, they are ready to launch forward into higher levels of craft, using punctuation as a deliberate tool in elevating sentence complexity and clarity. They are ready to shift text forms to suit their audience and purpose. They are ready to push themselves to more sophisticated vocabulary use, sentence structure, and paragraphing (Department of Education, Western Australia, 2006). These writers are ready to "master the mechanics" at a high level of proficiency that will infuse conventions into their thinking during drafting as well as while editing.

Writing is not necessarily neat and tidy. Let writers see how rereading and marking up a text can improve the quality of the writing.

Developing writers are ready to launch forward with punctuation as a deliberate tool in creating meaning.

The Importance of Approximation

While second and third graders usually have an arsenal of sound-symbol relationships and sight words that facilitate their work as writers, they still need to be encouraged to approximate spelling to keep their drafts focused on meaning and rich word choices. To validate the use of approximation, it is helpful to demonstrate strategies for approximating spelling.

These strategies for independence free writers to "keep writing," rather than getting stuck on the spelling of an unknown word. This is critical if we are to create resourceful and independent writers who realize that waiting in line for the teacher to provide the spelling of an unknown word will cause them to lose track of their thought and create an unnecessary dependency on the teacher that wastes learning time. But again, we must model…

Modeling Word Construction

While modeling word construction, we slowly and deliberately stretch out words, saying them slowly so we can hear the sounds. We model how to underline a word when we aren't feeling confident about its spelling. We model breaking a word into syllables and remembering that each syllable needs at least one vowel:

Writers, you are not only creating interesting writing that I am itching to read, you are getting better and better at breaking words into syllables to help yourselves spell. That is a very helpful strategy that I use while I am drafting and again when I am editing. Let's look together at this writing that I did a few days ago. I am going to think about the syllables in my words and check to be sure that I have at least one vowel for each syllable. I wrote, "It was a regular Saturday afternoon…" As I think about syllables, I don't need to check every word. Some words are very short some I am sure I spelled correctly. I am going to check *regular* and *afternoon*. *Reg/u/lar*. I hear three syllables. I will underline the vowels to check that I have a vowel in each syllable. Now, I will check *afternoon*. Think together. How many syllables in *afternoon*?

Spelling isn't just about correctness. It is also about developing a set of spelling strategies that enable a writer to problem-solve during drafting, notice when words are not spelled correctly during editing, and to establish a sense of spelling consciousness. A strategic speller applies spelling strategies throughout the writing process, crafting text with fluency and editing with an eye for convention.

Thinking About Audience

Developing writers in second and third grade have the capability of keeping their audience in mind as they draft, revise, and edit. This sense of audience adds strength to written text as the writer must constantly be rereading his or her work through the viewfinder of the reader. The writer must wonder if a reader will understand the message, be able to read the spelling, understand pause points and the flow of ideas. The writer must internally shift from writing for personal expression to writing with a reader in mind. When there is an authentic audience for their work, authors have strong and viable purposes for looking more closely at their work and expecting more from the print they create.

To build a sense of audience, we believe it is important to provide authentic reasons for students to share their writing. Activities such as partner sharing, author's chair, end-of-workshop sharing circles, and publishing all help. But we can go further. When writers have a clear understanding that their work will be public, mechanics and conventions become important in a personal way. The teacher as audience has, unfortunately, limited appeal. Editing and conventions utilized just to please the teacher quickly become tedious and boring.

> **❞ [With a focus on a reader] . . . the writer will have to take an idea and shape it with genre, form, sound, and the conventions of the language system all working together to produce a piece that has the desired impact on readers. ❞**
> —*Katie Wood Ray and Lisa Cleaveland*

Authentic audience and authentic purposes work hand in hand to provide motivation and a rationale for why conventions and mechanics are important. This is the time when we reread for "correctness" and for lifting the visual aspects of our message to the highest possible levels.

Ideas for Creating Authentic Audience

- Write notes to one another and the teacher.
- Write letters to their parents and ask the parents to write back.
- Write letters of request for travel brochures and mail them.
- Draft and edit a class newsletter that goes to parents at least once a month.
- Create partnerships with another class so writers can read their writing to another authentic audience.
- Publish class books and individual books.
- Create posters of processes and procedures for writing or classroom management.
- Post writing on the walls of the classroom that exemplify a specific craft element such as: Interesting Leads, Great Use of Interjections, Two-Word Sentences Mixed in With Longer Sentences, Finding Freedom From Fragments, Writing Transformed by Rereading.
- Create bulletin boards with sentence strips highlighting great moments in literature.

> **Famous Authors Draw a Reader's Attention With Sentence Openers Followed by a Comma...**

> **Favorite Authors Show Emotion: Interjections, Exclamations, and Caps for Emphasis...**

> **Fascinating Commas Found in Favorite Books**

- Provide "From the Desk of _____" pads and have students write notes for authentic purposes. (See Tools section, page 157.)
- Write get-well cards to fellow students and school personnel.
- Design interactive posters comparing the number of commas in *Amos and Boris* and *Shrek,* both by William Steig. Include sentence strips with favorite examples of sentences with interesting commas.

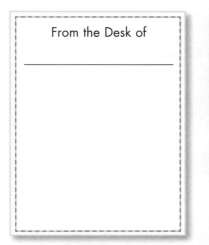

From the Desk of

_____

Second and third graders love to write notes. Why not encourage note writing with From the Desk of _____ forms. Students can write reminders to themselves, their friends, the teacher, or parents.

Authentic audiences build intrinsic motivation for improving the quality of mechanics and conventions.

I hope you get
better soon
so you can
rite your
books,

Here's hoping you're feeling better!

Get Well Soon

from Josh

In the summer before second grade, Josh Eitzen wrote this get-well note to a friend.

"Students can hear all we have to say about punctuation, but, if there are no real-life connections, little will stick.**"**
—Janet Angelillo

The Environment

The environment we create for writing is important. A rich environment for writing should have areas for the following activities.

Modeled writing and teacher think-aloud

Guided practice at an overhead or document camera

Editing conferences and coaching for individuals

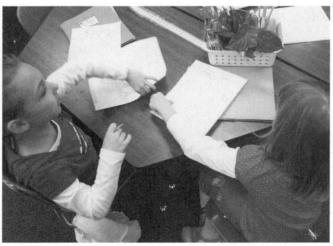

Partner editing

The walls should make strong statements about the learning in the classroom. Be sure modeled writing samples, word walls, editing checklists, and posters showing studies of conventions are clearly visible.

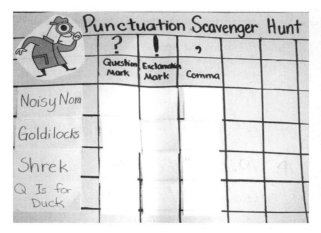

Word walls and lists of frequently used words should be positioned so that students can easily access the print.

Interactive posters built collaboratively with students make strong statements about the importance of conventions and mechanics in published literature and in our own work as writers.

Editing Checklist

Reread — Check over your writing
Make your writing reable.

☐ Use capitals → at the beginning of sentences My dog runs fast.
                    people's names Joseph Cecelia Mrs Hogan

☑ Use my best spelling. YES!!
☑ Mark words that don't look right. YES!!!
☑ NEVER, NEVER, NEVER EVER stop writing to ask how to
                                            spell a word.
                                    Keep those ideas flowing !!!

☑ Reread my writing and check for 1 thing at a time.

Editing checklists should emphasize your students' current phase of development and change over time to reflect new learning. Be sure to involve students in the development of the checklists so they have a voice in considering tools that support their writing.

With a grin of sheer delight, I lifed the warm, gooey cookie to my lips. Mmmm Good!

Pop! Sizzle! Zing! The heated kernels vibrated madly as they prepared to explode. Boom! Like a bomb, it goes kaboom.

Modeled writing should be available for children to revisit over time. It can become a source of familiar words and strategies as well as a resource to model continued editing and expansion of language.

Model the Use of Classroom Tools

When classroom walls reflect a rich tapestry of writing forms, tools, and supports, a strong message is sent to children, parents, and our colleagues that this is a classroom where writing and mechanics are celebrated and savored. It is important to remember, however, that rich visuals provide invitations, but real use will occur only with explicit and careful modeling of the tools in action.

> **Visuals are only helpful if students actively use them.**

We believe that we must model the use of word walls, charts, and environmental print so our students understand that as writers we select our tools carefully. Like a carpenter, we must select the tools that match our purposes and know when to use each one. During *prewriting,* we may turn to a mentor text for guidance on using commas in interesting ways or examine eye-catching punctuation in opening sentences. Our mentor texts may

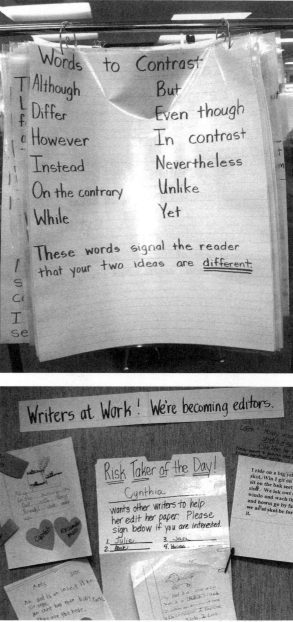

When student work is posted, it should be for a clear purpose that heightens awareness of conventions or elevates craft. Notice how this display invites editors to offer team support to a writer as she edits her work. This sets a model for collaborative thinking and heightens awareness of the importance of careful editing.

include modeled writing done by the teacher, the work of a peer, or a favorite picture book, such as *Owl Moon* by Jane Yolen.

During *drafting* we generally minimize tools, using portable word walls and class word walls only if we are sure we can find a word so quickly it won't interrupt our message.

When *editing* for an audience, we shift our stance and emphasize tools that will help us reach higher in our use of conventions and mechanics. This is the time when editing checklists, word walls, and other resources empower our thinking and help us to grow. Editing is also a time when we can view classmates as powerful resources and enter into editing partnerships.

When you take time to demonstrate and think aloud about your options for using tools while you are modeling writing for your students, they develop a deeper understanding of how tools empower and lift writing. Talk to writers about why you are or are not electing to turn to a resource or use a tool. Let them hear you be deliberate as you consider whether a tool will help you or distract you from your message. Let students hear you consider the use of a tool such as a class word wall, then decide to wait until editing. Let them see you walk to a tool such as a homophone chart while editing, then use the tool to consider a word choice. Tools are helpful resources *if* writers take an active stance in their use.

Class Lists of Conventions and Mechanics

Class editing posters that you add to with each cycle in this resource provide a cumulative record of your cycles. This keeps writers focused on what they have learned. This cumulative record of lessons is a powerful visual reminder to writers of their evolving control over print. With each cycle, you will notice that you are reminded to pause, review the class poster, and then add a new understanding. Because this list is displayed in a clearly visible place, writers can use it as a tool to assist their planning before drafting, as a reference while writing, or to support their thinking while editing.

Writing Folders and Personal Tools to Support Editors

Editors need personal tools, such as a well-organized writing folder in which they store their work and keep personal tools readily at hand. These personal tools might include topic lists, writer's notebooks, portable word walls, editing checklists, small dictionaries, and lists of skills that writers will be accountable to include in their completed pieces. Some classrooms even find that it is helpful to use the main writing folder for "pieces in progress" and warehouse previous writing pieces in a separate folder.

Skills I Can Use

In designing folders, we believe it is very helpful to keep a sheet of paper entitled "Skills I Can Use" attached to one side of the folder. This is a place to celebrate the accomplishments of each child. When we confer with a writer and observe that the child has correctly applied a convention or tool, we celebrate by writing the skill on the Skills I Can Use page and dating it.

This sheet becomes a record of the skills each individual learner can control as a writer. Each time we have an editing conference and

When writers have a well-organized writing folder, writing and personal tools are easily accessible.

Writing folders should have a place where learners can record "skills" or conventions they can use as writers. Once items are on their personal list, writers know they are accountable to work on their skills every time they edit. See Tools section, page 167, for a Skills I Can Use template.

work on a convention, a mechanic, or a spelling strategy, we add the skill to the Skills I Can Use list and date the entry. This list is an ongoing, personal reminder to the writer, the writer's editing partner, and the teacher of skills that have been mastered by each individual. Students learn that once a skill is added to their list, they take pride in their learning and know they are now accountable for applying the skill in every piece of writing that will have an audience.

Remember Focused Edits

Simultaneous rereading for every element on a checklist can be too great of a challenge and result in less effective editing. Each item on an editing checklist should get its own focused edit. If there are four items on the checklist, writers will reread at least four times.

We like to encourage the following steps, modeled after Day 2 of our editing cycles, for "Partner Editing for an Audience":

1. The author reads his or her piece to a partner or partners.

2. The partner(s) offer a compliment about the message.

3. The partner(s) and the author together begin a series of focused edits using an editing checklist.

4. The team then decides if they want to invite in another editor for a last round of edits or if they believe the piece is ready to present to the teacher for a teacher editing conference.

Editing Checklists

The goal of editing checklists is to teach students to take responsibility to reread and be their own first editors. The checklist, in combination with Skills I Can Use pages and class editing posters, scaffolds learners for success. Checklists are tools that support students' use of known skills. They do not provide instruction.

Just as we differentiate in other areas of the curriculum, personal editing checklists can provide further opportunity to scaffold and support learners across the range of diverse texts in your classroom. We encourage you to explore the checklists in the Assessment and Record Keeping section of this resource, pages 160–175. While these examples may offer matches to some of your students, please also consider creating your own editing checklists that match up precisely with the *Mastering the Mechanics* cycles you have selected for instruction.

> **It is important to remember that editing checklists do not "teach," they simply remind students to use the processes that you have modeled.**

Checklists for Partner Editing

Once writers review their work on their own, they are ready to engage in partner edits. During partner editing, writers collaboratively use editing checklists and their shared sense of language and convention to lift a piece to a level that an individual writer may not have reached alone.

Creating Checklists With Your Students

When students are involved in creating editing checklists, they must reflect on what they know about conventions and mechanics, then design tools that will help them to be accountable for what they know. We believe strongly in having students work with us in whole-class and small group settings to design editing checklists that match phases of development or apply to a specific kind of writing. The ownership and empowerment fostered by learner-developed editing checklists changes writers.

The Teaching/Assessing Loop

Assessment is our essential guide to quality instruction. As we observe writers during drafting, meeting with them in small groups or conferring with individuals, we are constantly assessing to determine what they do and do not know. Our assessments are the best possible guides to instruction. The data we gather through thoughtful assessment help us choose the next skills our students need and also helps us determine whether our students are fully grasping the material we're teaching.

Selecting Editing Skills for Instruction

To determine which conventions and mechanics are expected at your grade level, look first at your state standards. We suggest that you consider highlighting these standards on a photocopy of the Skills Continuum, located on pages 34–38. If you are working with a mandated language arts resource, you might identify the skills for spelling, punctuation, grammar, and so on in the program, then highlight those on the grid as well. (We like to add program-driven goals in a second color so we can see where they deviate from state standards.) Now, as you look at the grid, you have a unified picture that shows state standards and program requirements in a single, easy-to-follow format that will round out your editing work with second- and third-grade writers. Then, assess the skills your students are already implementing in their writing.

Assess the Skills Your Students Can Use

We find it immensely helpful to collect *unedited* writing samples and use the Class Record-Keeping Grid provided in the Assessment and Record Keeping section, page 170. It only takes minutes to list student names in the first column and jot target conventions and mechanics across the top of the other columns. With a stack of writing samples in hand, you are ready to start placing checkmarks for writers whose work demonstrates adequate space between words, periods, capitals, and so on.

Assessment leads the way to quality instruction.

Once you have a profile of your students and their needs, you are ready to select a cycle and start "Mastering the Mechanics"!

In the "How an Octopus…" example below, our assessment review shows this writer using some transition words to link ideas (*first*, *then*). The sentences are complete. One sentence, "When

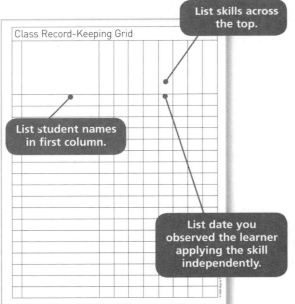

List skills across the top.

List student names in first column.

List date you observed the learner applying the skill independently.

Helpful tip: Photocopy the Class Record-Keeping Grid after you have entered student names in the first column and you will be ready to gather data on a wide variety of skills without having to write student names each time.

How An Octopus Protects Herself

An octopus has many ways to protect herself. First she can take her eight legs and wrap them around other animals. She can use the suction cups on her legs to grip things. When an animal tries to attack her, she can make her body squish together so she can hide out in little places. That was a surprise to me! An octopus can squirt ink into the water and blind the attacker for a little bit of time. Then she swims off. Pretty cool. ways to protect herself

by Stephanie J.

Notice that Teresa uses the clipboard and grid during writing conferences and when moving around the room to assist writers.

an animal tries to attack her,…" uses a strong opening with a comma to draw in the reader. This writer/editor would benefit from work on paragraphs and headings, which are conventions of organization that make informational text more manageable for a reader. So to fill out the chart, we could place a tally or date observed under transition words, openers with a comma, and complete sentences. Since this is only one example, we would make a point to collect more evidence that these skills have truly been mastered.

With the support of the grid, we quickly expose patterns of strength as well as need for individuals, small groups, and the class as a whole. The grid allows us to identify groups of writers who share similar needs and to easily gather small groups for explicit instruction. We find this assessment so helpful that we keep it on a clipboard while circulating during writer's workshop and during writing conferences.

Notice Oral Language Patterns

Grammar in student writing is tightly linked to oral language. With this in mind, we challenge ourselves to listen carefully and try to notice which students need support with subject–verb agreement, verb tenses, or the use of pronouns in oral speech. You may hear your students using oral patterns such as "My mom, she went to the store," "Me and Bobby raced on our skateboards," and "We don't have no paper towels." Record your observations and compare the patterns you notice in oral language with those in your students' writing. This provides a balanced assessment of oral and written language use that can help you make critical decisions about which cycles to select. If you have only a small group of students for whom grammatical structures are an issue, you may elect to differentiate by engaging a small group in a cycle directly targeted to its needs. If many of your students are having the same difficulty, selecting the grammar cycles on this topic may be the perfect choice for the entire class. Again, assessment leads the way to quality instruction.

Supporting and Respecting

We must always respect home language and community culture, yet we have a responsibility to help learners understand and apply the more formal registers of English that are seen in published books and expected of proficient writers. While we would never show disrespect to language patterns that are native to the children, it may be helpful to explain to students that language shifts to match the audience. For example, we speak to the principal or a police officer differently than we do to our friends on the playground. There are certain "formal" registers of language that we are expected to use as writers that aren't always expected when we talk to our friends or relax in our homes.

To support conventional grammar use, we can highlight conventional grammar in our favorite books, think aloud about grammar while crafting sentences during modeled writing, or respond with elaborated language when students use nonstandard structures. The trick to elaborating and extending language use is to mirror the learner's message using correct form in your response. There is no reprimand for incorrect usage, you simply mirror what the student has said by restating it in conventional form.

A few examples:

If a student says:	You might reply:
Last night we goed to the ballpark.	You *went* to the ballpark! How lucky for you.
Me and my dad went fishing.	My *dad and I* used to go fishing, too. Did you have a wonderful time?
My sister, she fell and broke her arm.	*Your sister fell* and broke her arm! How awful. How is she doing?
We don't got no paper towels.	We don't *have any* paper towels? Would you like to write a note to the custodian so he knows?
I seen a car crash this morning.	You *saw* a crash? I hope everyone is okay.

Editing Conferences:
Adding the Chocolate Swirls

Assuming that you have already held a revision conference with the writer, an editing conference provides a second opportunity for you and the writer to think together about a piece of writing. The first time, the emphasis was on meaning, which may have included the use of interesting punctuation to lift the writing. This time the focus of the conference is on editing.

During this conference, select one or two skills to address with the student. Never teach more than one or two things, as the writer is not likely to be able to retain more information. We like to keep sticky notes on hand during editing conferences, as we believe that when writers make their own corrections and retain control of the pencil, they are more likely to remember and reuse what they have learned. By jotting down suggested edits on sticky notes, writers retain control of the pen and understand that they have a responsibility to edit their own work. During an editing conference, the writer has responsibility for his or her actions. This isn't about teacher corrections. It is about writers moving forward in their use of conventions and mechanics.

With this in mind, an editing conference might sound something like this:

> Anna, you must be so pleased that you have decided to publish your piece on giving your dog a bath. As a reader, I could totally visualize the soapy mess that you AND the dog became during this particular bath. What a great job you did in explaining the bubbles and the water.
>
> As we begin editing, please tell me what you and your editing partner have already discovered and worked on in your writing. Be sure to point out any changes or additions you and your editing partner were able to make.
>
> I see that you have underlined six words that you want to look at for spelling. Please show me the two you most want to work on today. Great! Let's look closely at *soapy* and *fur*. I will use these sticky notes to write the correct spelling for these words and place them on your paper so you can finish editing the spelling after our conference.

Steps for Editors When Writing for an Audience

We teach writers that if they are going to have an audience for their writing, they need to follow these last steps as editors:

1. Use an editing checklist to do a focused edit for each item on the list.

2. Find an editing partner. Read the writing together and think about making it the best it can be.

3. Sign up for an editing conference with the teacher.

A Note About the Yearlong Planner

The sample Yearlong Planner featured on the gatefold (the inside front cover) of this book is a tool to help you map out your curriculum for mechanics and conventions for the year. As you can see, this planner provides week-by-week suggestions for three content cycles followed by a Pulling It All Together cycle to solidify the learning with authentic, interactive purposes. During a Pulling It All Together cycle, no new skills are added. This is a time for learners to apply their learning from the previous cycles in authentic contexts. With this plan as your guide, students will have four weeks of instruction and plentiful opportunities to transfer skills to long-term memory.

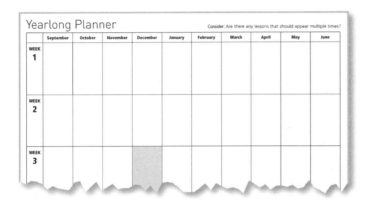

Please note that on page 159, a blank version of the Yearlong Planner is provided. With this planner, you can use your informal assessments along with your state standards to build a personalized curriculum map.

Important Note: The sample planner does not contain all of the lessons in this resource. We built a wide range of lessons to support your responses to the needs of your students. There are many paths through this resource. You may elect to use all of the planner, or portions of it, or you can select lessons entirely based upon the needs of your learners. The choices and the path you select are up to you.

On Your Way!

The cycles that are the centerpiece of this resource are meant to celebrate writers and their ever-growing control over craft and form. As you enter these cycles, we challenge you to recast conventions and mechanics as tools for enhancing meaning and to have a joyous journey as you "Master the Mechanics."

PART II

Skills
Continuum

The skills continuum profiles the spectrum of development in mechanics and conventions that might be expected from learners in the elementary grades. For ease of use, it is divided into sections that match the organizational structure of the lessons.

Each convention listed on the continuum is supported by an explanation that often includes an example for clarity. To the right of each listed convention and example is a designation of grade level(s) at which writers should be exposed to and learn to implement the convention. When a convention is supported by a lesson in this resource, the page number on which the lesson appears is also listed.

You may find it helpful to photocopy the continuum and keep a copy on a clipboard to serve as:

- a quick reference when planning your own mini-lessons or cycles of support for conventions

- a source of support when conferring with students during writing conferences

- a place to highlight and date when you provide mini-lessons on a convention

Overall, the continuum should offer a broad-based view of your students' writing development across the range of mechanics, conventions, and processes that good editors use and empower your thinking as you differentiate instruction for the range of learners you serve.

> **Sections of the Continuum**
> Processes Editors Use
> Capitalization
> Grammar
> Punctuation
> Spacing
> Spelling

Page where lesson appears in this book	Conventions & Mechanics	Explanation	K	1	2	3	4	5
	PROCESSES EDITORS USE							
	Putting your name on the paper	Writers should habitualize writing their names on papers before creating text or drawings.	•	•				
	Counting the words in a message	Before writing, young writers count the words in their message to match speech to print.	•	•				
	Reread and touch each word	Writers touch each word to check for omissions.	•	•	•			
	Reread to focus on message	Meaning is always our first emphasis when creating text. Writers must reread to confirm or revise for meaning before focusing on surface conventions.	•	•	•	•	•	•
	Reread to edit for conventions	Once meaning is clear, writers reread to check for surface structures and grammar that give our writing uniformity.	•	•	•	•	•	•
40	**Focused edit: reread for each editing point**	Rereading helps writers check for surface structures and grammar. The piece is read once for each editing point.	•	•	•	•	•	•
42	**Use an editing checklist**	Checklists matched to developmental levels of writers are used to guide personal and partner edits.	•	•	•	•	•	•
44	**Use copyediting symbols to support editing**	Authors and editing partners use standardized copyediting symbols to identify and support their editorial work.				•	•	•
	Edit with a partner	When partners work together to proofread, they elevate each other's thinking about text.	•	•	•	•	•	•
	Celebrate and self-reflect	To grow, writers must take time to reflect on their own growth as communicators of meaning.	•	•	•	•	•	•
	CAPITALIZATION							
	Capitalize the pronoun "I"	I am going to Anna's house.	•	•	•	•	•	•
	Use mostly lowercase letters	Capital letters need to be used for specific purposes.	•	•				
	Capitalize the beginning of sentences	Capitalize the first word in each sentence.	•	•	•	•	•	•
50	**Capitalize proper nouns: names, places, things**	My sister, Anna, is taking dance lessons in Seattle. She hopes to perform at the Keller Auditorium.	•	•	•	•	•	•
	Capitalize a title before a name	Mrs. Jones works in the office of Judge Jacobs.	•	•	•	•	•	•
	Capitalize proper adjectives	Proper adjectives are formed from a noun used as an adjective: American figure skaters; French bread.				•	•	•
	Capitalize days of the week	Monday, Tuesday	•	•	•	•	•	•
	Capitalize titles and headings	*Where the Wild Things Are, My Swimming Party*	•	•	•	•	•	•
48	**Capitalize for emphasis**	HOORAY!			•	•	•	•
	Capitalize AM and PM	Abbreviations for morning and afternoon need to be capitalized when they are written without a period.			•	•	•	•
	Capitalize abbreviations for state names (OR, CA, NY)	Names of states are abbreviated with two capital letters.			•	•	•	•

	Common nouns can become proper nouns	A common noun, used as a name of a person, is capitalized when there is no possessive or article preceding it. Grandma and Mom went shopping. Grandma and my mom went shopping.			•	•	•	•

GRAMMAR

56	**Complete sentences**	Writers avoid unintentional sentence fragments (The fuzzy puppy) and need to acquire a strong foundation in writing complete, interesting sentences (The fuzzy puppy howled at the moon.).	•	•	•	•	•	•
	Phrase	A phrase is a group of words that takes the place of a specific part of speech. *The house at the end of the street* is a phrase that acts like a noun. The phrase *at the end of the street* is a prepositional phrase that acts like an adjective.			•	•	•	•
	Clause	A clause is a word or group of words ordinarily consisting of a subject and a predicate. A clause usually contains a verb and may or may not be a sentence in its own right. (Example: I didn't know that the cat ran up the tree. *That the cat ran up the tree* is a clause. This clause includes the phrase *up the tree*.)					•	•
58	**Sentence parts: simple subject and simple verb**	Writers understand the essential components of a sentence, the who or what does something (subject) and what the subject does (verb). Toddlers scamper. Brian cheered.		•	•	•	•	•
	Control sentence length vs. run-on sentences	Writers use simple, compound, or complex sentences to enrich writing, while avoiding run-ons. Nonstandard: The fuzzy puppy snuggled in my arms and then he ate fast and played and barked and then he. . . Standard: The fuzzy puppy, while snuggling in my arms, fell quickly asleep. Then, he. . .		•	•	•	•	•
88	**Use transition words**	Transition words are used to organize writing and alert readers to changes in the text. (Finally, our long-awaited order arrived.)	•	•	•	•	•	•
	Singular and plural nouns	Writers understand the difference between singular and plural nouns, and can form plurals.	•	•	•	•	•	•
64	**Single vs. double subject**	Writers avoid the nonstandard double subject (My mom she prefers. . .) and select single subjects for sentences (My mom prefers. . .).	•	•	•	•	•	•
66	**Singular subject-verb agreement**	A singular noun and pronoun (subject) agrees with its verb in number, case, and person. (Singular: Mary giggles.)	•	•	•	•	•	•
68	**Plural subject-verb agreement**	Plural nouns and pronouns (subjects) agree with their verbs in number, case, and person. (Plural: The babies wobble.)	•	•	•	•	•	•
78	**Present- and Past-tense verbs**	Writers differentiate between present- and past-tense verbs to show *when* an action takes place. (I sit on the edge of my bed. I sat on the edge of my bed.)	•	•	•	•	•	•
	Verb tense: future	Writers expand their use of verbs to show a future action or state of being. (Mario will be a stellar teacher.)	•	•	•	•	•	•
	Verb types: action	The most common verb is the action verb that tells what the subject is doing. (Mario swims across the lake.)	•	•	•	•	•	•
76	**Verb types: linking**	Writers use linking verbs (nonaction verbs) to connect the subject with nouns, pronouns, or adjectives after the linking verbs: *is, are, was, were*. (Margarita is my maternal aunt.)	•	•	•	•	•	•
	Verb types: main	When a verb is composed of two or more words, the verb at the end of the verb phrase is the main (principal) verb. (Anna is dancing down the hall.)			•	•	•	•
76	**Verb types: helping**	Writers use helping (auxiliary) verbs to create verb phrases that consist of a helping verb and the main (principal) verb. (Anna is dancing down the hall.)			•	•	•	•
	Verb forms: regular	Most verbs are regular. Writers add *-ed* to show a past action, or use a helping verb (*has, had, have*).			•	•	•	•

Page	Skill	Description						
	Verb forms: irregular	Some verbs are irregular. Their past-tense form is not made by adding -ed or when using helping verbs. Past tense is expressed with a new word (run, ran).			•	•	•	•
62	**Pronoun order (person's name and then I, not me)**	Standard form: My mom and I. . . My mom, dad, and I. . . Nonstandard: Me and my mom. Me and my dad and my mom. . .	•	•	•	•	•	•
60	**Pronouns and the nouns to which they refer (their antecedents)**	Writers identify the nouns to which pronouns refer. Standard: Niva is an exceptional cook. She whipped up dinner last night. Nonstandard: She is an exceptional cook. She whipped up dinner last night.		•	•	•	•	•
	Possessive pronouns	Possessive pronouns take the place of a noun and show ownership. Most possessive pronouns are written without an apostrophe (my, our, their).	•	•	•	•	•	•
	Subjective and objective cases of pronouns and nouns	Nouns remain the same for both subjective and objective cases, whereas pronouns require differentiation between the subjective (I, you, he, she, it, we, you, they) and objective (me, you, him, her, it, us, you, them) cases.				•	•	•
	Double negatives	Only one word should be used to express a negative idea. Frequent errors occur when writers use not with never, no, hardly, and so on. Standard: We don't have any paper towels. Nonstandard: We don't got no paper towels.				•	•	•
70	**Adjectives to Lift Descriptions**	Writers include adjectives, words that describe nouns and pronouns, to strengthen text. (The brilliant butterfly zipped past the decrepit barn.)	•	•	•	•	•	•
72	**Adjectives: comparative and superlative forms**	Adjectives can be used to compare two or more people, places, things, or ideas (examples: bigger, biggest; more/less helpful; most/least helpful).			•	•	•	•
	Articles	Articles are adjectives. The indicates a specific (definite) article. (Bring me the striped sweater.) A and an refer to no particular thing. A is used before a consonant sound. (Bring me a sweater.) An is used before a vowel sound. (Bring me an apple.)		•	•	•	•	•
74	**Adverbs and adverb phrases**	Adverbs modify verbs, adjectives, or other adverbs. Most adverbs tell when, where, how, and to what extent/degree. (Marcos quickly zipped over the goal line.)			•	•	•	•
	Adverbs: comparative and superlative forms	Adverbs can be used to compare two or more people, places, things, or ideas. (Examples: faster, fastest; more/less carefully, most/least carefully)				•	•	•
	Interjections	Interjections are words or phrases that are used to express a strong emotion and are separated from the rest of the sentence by a comma or an exclamation point. (Wow! This is cool! Wow, this is cool!)	•	•	•	•	•	•
	Prepositions and prepositional phrases	Prepositions are not modifiers; their function is to relate a noun or pronoun to another word in the sentence. A prepositional phrase includes a preposition, the object of the preposition, and any modifiers. (The cat snoozed under the lawn chair.)			•	•	•	•
	Conjunctions: coordinate	Conjunctions connect words or groups of words. Coordinate conjunctions connect equal parts: words, phrases, and independent clauses (sentences). Examples of coordinating conjunctions: for, and, nor, but, or, yet, so.			•	•	•	•
	Conjunctions: subordinate	Conjunctions connect words or groups of words. Subordinate conjunctions connect two clauses to make complex sentences. Examples of subordinating conjunctions: after, because, before, until, when, while.			•	•	•	•

PUNCTUATION

Page	Skill	Example	1	2	3	4	5	6
82	**Periods: end of sentence**	Declarative sentences need a period at the end.	•	•	•	•	•	•
	Period with abbreviation	Mr. Jones; a.m. or p.m.			•	•	•	•
82	**Exclamation points: exclamatory sentences and interjections**	An exclamation point is used for emphasis. Examples: Drip! Drop! I can't believe it is still raining!	•	•	•	•	•	•
82	**Question marks: interrogative sentences**	Question marks are placed at the end of sentences that inquire.	•	•	•	•	•	•
84	**Commas: use in a series**	I need to buy shoes, socks, an umbrella, and a jacket.		•	•	•	•	•
	Comma to separate day, and year	December 28, 2008		•	•	•	•	•
	Comma to separate city and state	Portland, Oregon		•	•	•	•	•
88	**Comma following a transition word at the beginning of sentences**	Finally, our long-awaited order arrived.		•	•	•	•	•
94	**Comma precedes a connecting word (coordinate conjunction) when combining two short sentences**	Anna has my library book, and Devon has my lunch. (Examples of connecting words: *so, or, but, and*)		•	•	•	•	•
	Comma with direct address	Anna, grab your coat!			•	•	•	•
	Commas in a letter	Place a comma after the greeting and the closing.		•	•	•	•	•
	Comma surrounds an appositive	Anna, the amazing runner, won the medal.			•	•	•	•
86	**Comma: After introductory phrase or clause**	When they heard the final bell, the children headed for the bus.			•	•	•	•
	Comma to set off closer	The children tiptoed down the hall, wondering what would happen next.					•	•
96	**Punctuation in dialogue**	"Hurry up!," cried Anna. "Can you help me find my keys?" her mother asked.	•	•	•	•	•	•
90	**Apostrophes: contraction**	Can't, won't, shouldn't	•	•	•	•	•	•
92	**Apostrophes: Possessives**	Anna's bike is bright yellow.	•	•	•	•	•	•
	Colon in reporting the time	10:30 a.m.			•	•	•	•
	Colon at the beginning of a list	They had a long list of errands, including the following: going to the grocery store, the post office, and the health food store.			•	•	•	•
	Hyphen to join compound descriptions	Heavy-handed dog trainer; father-in-law.				•	•	•
	Hyphen to separate syllables	At the end of a line, if there isn't room for the entire word, syllables are separated with a hyphen.				•	•	•
	Underline or italicize a book title	When a book or play title is handwritten, it should be underlined.				•	•	•
	Ellipses	Use ellipses to indicate a pause in thought, or the omission of words or sentences. Example: I won't go, but. . .				•	•	•

CONVENTIONS FOR SPACING

			C1	C2	C3	C4	C5	C6
	Word boundaries: keep letters in a word close together	Letters in a word need to be clustered so word boundaries are apparent.	•	•				
	Using entire page	Writers should write from top to bottom, left to right, using return sweep.	•	•				
	Using multiple pages	Writers need to expand their thinking beyond single-page writing experiences.	•	•	•	•	•	•
	Margins	Allow appropriate margin, header, and footer spaces.	•	•	•	•	•	•
102	Pagination in a multiple-page piece	Page breaks are governed by arrangement around visuals and by available space on a page. Each page in a story should have a page number.	•	•	•	•	•	•
102	Spacing of visuals in non-fiction	Visuals carry important messages in nonfiction and can appear in many positions on a page.	•	•	•	•	•	•
	Placement of nonfiction features	Nonfiction features such as the table of contents, captions, headings, index, and glossary have their own conventions for spacing.	•	•	•	•	•	•
	Paragraph breaks	Paragraphs should be arranged on a page so they are clearly set apart from one another.				•	•	•
100	Spacing in a letter	Spacing for friendly and business letters follows a uniform format for the date, greeting, closing, and signature.			•	•	•	•
	Spacing on an envelope	Envelopes have clearly defined spaces for the addressee and the return address.			•	•	•	•

SPELLING

			C1	C2	C3	C4	C5	C6
106	Spelling consciousness	Students should have a high level of awareness that spelling is important.	•	•	•	•	•	•
	Stretching words	Writers say words slowly to pull them apart auditorily.	•	•	•	•	•	•
	Reread to add more letters	Rereading allows writers opportunities to modify spelling.	•	•	•			
	Big words have more letters than small words	Writers need to expect to use more letters in longer words as they develop spelling consciousness.	•	•				
	Spelling reference: picture alphabet card	Picture alphabet cards help writers identify sound-symbol relationships.	•	•				
	Spelling reference: portable word wall	Word walls help writers quickly access high-frequency words. Content word walls support spelling of content-specific words.	•	•	•	•	•	•
	Use known words to spell other words.	Spelling by analogy allows students to use known words and word parts to spell other words. If I can write *in*, then I can also write *pin*.	•	•	•	•	•	•
108	Noticing syllables: each syllable needs a vowel	Writers need to expect to place at least one vowel in every syllable.	•	•	•	•	•	
110	Try different spellings for words	When faced with an uncertain spelling, writers benefit from trying various spellings in the margin or on a separate sheet of paper.		•	•	•	•	•
	Homophones	Homophones are words that sound the same but have different spellings and meanings (*their*, *there*, *they're*; *no*, *know*)		•	•	•	•	•

Rereading for multiple purposes helps writers look closely at meaning and conventions.

Lesson Cycles for Mastering the Mechanics

Cycles for Understanding the Editing Process

Writers need to consider mechanics and conventions as tools to lift their messages, clarify meaning, and focus their editing as they prepare for an audience.

Rereading is a tool that supports writers at every phase of the drafting and editing processes. It is, unquestionably, our greatest tool for supporting the editing process.

- Writers need to reread constantly. They reread to confirm their message, to regain momentum, and to consider what to say next. They reread to think about letters, sounds, and word choice. They reread to edit or to make sure they have placed their name on the paper.

- Editing checklists guide writers and editing partners in rereading for conventions and mechanics.

- Focused edits engage writers in a process of rereading once for each editing point.

Reread During Writing and Editing

DAY 1   Model the Focus Point

Rereading is one of the most important things writers do. While I am writing, I reread to see how it sounds. If I notice a mistake or a place where I missed a word, I quickly fix it, and then reread to check myself. Rereading during writing helps me keep up my momentum and focus on ideas. After I finish a piece of writing, I will reread even more carefully! My first sentence starts with *Good dads are hard to beat. . . .* I am going to reread and check what I have written so far. [After writing] **My ideas are pretty much in place, so this rereading is a time to check carefully for mistakes in spelling, capitalization, punctuation, and grammar. This kind of reread is called proofreading. Proofreading is a time when we read to edit or fix mistakes.**

> **Modeled Writing Sample**
>
> A Blue Ribbon Dad
>
> Good dads are hard to beat, especially when the dad is an emperor penguin. After a mother penguin lays her egg, she carefully places the egg on the father's feet and walks away. She doesn't just take a short stroll, she walks for a hundred miles to reach the ocean and find food!

 TURN AND TALK What did you notice about the two types of rereading you saw me do? How are they the same? In what ways are they different?

 SUM IT UP Reread during writing to keep up your momentum and focus on meaning. After writing, reread to carefully proofread and edit.

DAY 2   Guided Practice

Display student writing using a writing sample from page 188 in the appendix or from your class. If the author is one of your students, invite the author to read the selection to the class.

> **the dark**
>
> Some people fear the dark
>
> Darkness has the power to make you feel alone. Without light, your imagination can make you think that harmless things are suddenly scary.
>
> Things are different for nocturnal animals.
>
> Nocturnal animals love the dark because they can see very well. Their eyes are especially large and can reflect even small amounts of light back into the eye.

 TURN AND TALK
- First, discuss the meaning of the piece; then give compliments about the writing.

- Now, read over the writing. What is the evidence that the writer most likely reread either during or after writing? Finally, together, carefully reread to proofread and offer suggestions for editing.

 SUM IT UP To a class editing chart, add "Reread during and after writing."

Remember, rereading is important. Reread while you write and again to proofread and edit.

DAY 3 **Independent Practice**

Look through a writing folder and select writing to reread for multiple purposes, modeling how you reread to think about meaning, then reread again to proofread and edit. Give student editors a few minutes to replicate your modeling, proofreading and editing their own work.

 PEER EDIT Talk with your partner about the number of times you reread and your purpose for each rereading. Point out what you noticed while rereading. Were you able to make any changes? Exchange papers and proofread each other's papers.

 SUM IT UP Writers reread during writing as well as at the end of writing, when they proofread and edit.

✔ Assess the Learning

- Use a class record-keeping grid as you observe editors at work. Identify writers who reread during drafting as well as those who methodically proofread and edit after writing.

- Ask editors to list the different aspects of writing (for example: capitalization of proper nouns, commas in a series) that they think they can successfully proofread and edit, and those that are still a challenge.

Link the Learning

- Have writers practice rereading for multiple purposes as they create a math story problem or an observation in a science notebook. Encourage rereading during drafting and then careful rereading to proofread and edit. Have partners double-check each other's work.

- Those who do not yet have this understanding can be gathered into a brief guided writing experience where you might again model and guide rereading during and after writing.

- Model rereading for multiple purposes in several genres of writing so writers see how rereading helps across many types of texts.

- Have writers place sticky notes on their desk and tally each time they reread. This encourages them to be highly conscious of rereading. Guide writers in talking about the "during" writing reasons to reread. Then, have writers reread to edit and again focus consciously on their purposes before sharing their thinking with others.

Use an Editing Checklist

DAY 1   **Model the Focus Point**

Note: Select a piece of writing from a previous modeled writing sample and prepare a chart listing items for an editing checklist. (See editing checklists on pages 161–164.)

> **Editing checklists, like this one, help us keep track of our proofreading and editing. I am going to reread this writing for the purpose of editing. That is called proofreading. I am going to proofread for spelling first. I will place my hands around each word to help me look closely at spelling. Placing my hands around each word really helps! Looking at one word at a time helps me proofread.** (Finish reading for spelling.) **Now that I have checked for spelling, I am ready to proofread for another purpose. The checklist says** *Sentence opener followed by a comma.* **Look, my first sentence has a sentence opener and comma! I can check that one off. This editing checklist helps a lot. Let's keep going.**

> **Modeled Writing Sample**
>
> **Rulers of the Sea**
>
> Just as humans rule the land, sharks rule the sea! Their ferocious attacks occur with no warning and leave victims with little chance for escape. Clear blue waters and rolling surf may be beautiful, but they are also the hunting grounds of one of the world's most dangerous creatures.

TURN AND TALK Discuss how using an editing checklist can help you proofread and edit.

SUM IT UP After writing, use a checklist to proofread and edit one editing point at a time.

DAY 2   **Guided Practice**

Use the writing sample from page 176 or one from your class to display on the overhead. If the author is one of your students, invite the author to read the selection to the class.

TURN AND TALK Discuss the meaning of the writing and give the author compliments about the writing. Partners, I am giving you an editing checklist to support your proofreading. Use it to think together about this writing. You will read the piece one time for each item on the checklist. Be prepared to make suggestions for the author.

SUM IT UP To a class editing chart, add "Use an editing checklist."

Remember, use a checklist to proofread and edit after you have finished writing.

> My fat Tail Lepord Gray Geko has a fat tail. I hold hime every day. Some times he climes on my bed. his name is Jake. hise favorit thing to eat is meal worms. He lives in a ten golen fish tanck. He has a lot of room. Bhise favorit things to do are eat slepe a stae still.

DAY 3 | **Independent Practice**

Use selected writing from a writing folder to model how to use a checklist to proofread and edit for one aspect of writing at a time. Model rereading the piece for each item on the checklist. Give writers a few minutes to use their checklists to proofread and edit.

 PEER EDIT Think about what you did when you used the checklist. Then, point out places where you edited your writing. Share your thinking about proofreading, editing, and the checklist.

 SUM IT UP When we are writing for an audience, editing checklists help us to proofread carefully. The key is to check for one editing item at a time.

✓ Assess the Learning

- Have students write a letter to their parents explaining how to use a checklist to proofread and edit for one aspect of writing at a time after completing a piece. Assess letters for student understanding.

- Type a portion of familiar shared reading material with added errors in punctuation, capitalization, spelling, or grammar. Have writers use a checklist to proofread and edit. Assess for student understanding.

∞ Link the Learning

- Volunteer your students as "proofreaders" for another class. Have them take their checklists and partner with a peer from a different room to teach the other student how to use the checklist effectively.

- Have partners interview administrators, teachers, and students, asking, "What are the words you misspell most often?" Make a list of the words most often misspelled and have students challenge themselves to learn those words.

- Create a "Writing Under Construction" bulletin board spotlighting papers where errors were caught using a checklist to proofread and edit for one focus point at a time. Celebrate the role checklists play in helping us make our writing readable to others.

- Work with students to create a class editing checklist that matches your purposes for a particular piece of writing.

Use Copyediting Symbols

DAY 1 Model the Focus Point

Note: Prepare this writing in advance and have an enlarged copy of *Copy Editor's Symbols* from page 156 for the students to view.

> Copy editors are responsible for checking writing to be sure it is error-free before it is published. Every book in our library was edited by its writer, perhaps by an editing partner, and then finally by a copy editor. Today I am going to read this like a copy editor and use editing symbols to tell the author what needs to be changed. In the first sentence, I am noticing that Pecos Bill is a name. Names need capital letters. Watch as I draw three little lines under *p* in Pecos and *b* in Bill to tell this author these need to be capitals. I am looking at *ciotese*. I think that should be *coyotes* so I will write a little /sp/ next to this word to tell the author this needs to be fixed. Next, I am looking for the end of the sentence. There should be a period after *him* for the end of the sentence. It isn't there. The copy editor's symbol for "insert a period" is a circle with a little dot inside. Let's review my copyediting of this sentence. What do the marks tell the author to do?

Modeled Writing Sample

Pecos Bill, The Cowboy Folk Hero

When pecos bill was baby,
he fell out of his parents
                    sp
wagon and some cioetese
found him⊙

- - - - - - - - - - - - - - - - - - - -

        sp
They rased him like he was
    sp
there pup and taught him to
live in the wild.

 TURN AND TALK What did you notice about the copyediting marks? How might they assist our work as writers? How might we use them to help each other?

 SUM IT UP Copy editors use symbols to help authors identify changes that need to be made in a piece of writing. Published pieces need to be error-free.

DAY 2 Guided Practice

Use the Dear Mrs. Hoyt letter from page 177 or a writing sample from your class. If the author is one of your students, invite the author to read the selection to the class.

 TURN AND TALK Note: Make student copies of Copy Editor's Symbols on page 156.

> Talk about the meaning of the writing and share a compliment, too. Partners, your job is to think together. If you were to help this author with this writing, which copyediting symbols would you use and where would you put them?

Dear Mrs. Hoyt,
   Thank you for everything.
I loved the way you did
things also I liked the web
of undurstanding it was cool. I had
fun with everything. I hope you
have a good trip Home to oregon.
                 Love,
                 Kala
Read books,

 SUM IT UP To a class editing chart, add "Use copyediting symbols."

DAY 3 | Independent Practice

Make multiple copies of a piece of student writing from your class or from the samples in this resource. Have editing partners insert copyediting symbols into the piece, and then create teams of four to discuss the symbols they used, why they placed them where they did, and so on.

 PEER EDIT Partners, today you are working together as copy editors for this piece of writing. Insert the copyediting marks and prepare to share your thinking with another team. Listen for the signal so you will know it is time to cluster into groups of four.

 SUM IT UP Copyediting marks tell writers where editing is needed and what needs to be done.

✔ Assess the Learning

- Have students select a piece to publish and use copyediting symbols as they take the piece through a personal edit, a peer edit, and, finally, a teacher edit. Document how proficient the writer was in utilizing the symbols and then editing.

- Observe or interview writers as they edit a paper marked with copyediting symbols. Identify students who need more support in using the symbols.

🔗 Link the Learning

- Have partners exchange papers and use copyediting symbols to proofread and mark each other's papers. Return papers so authors can edit their own work.

- Create a bulletin board with copyediting symbols at the center. Post it in the hallway so your students can teach friends from other classes how to use the symbols.

- Volunteer your students to be coaches for another class so they can teach someone else how to use copyediting symbols.

- Have your students write and publish a class newsletter to distribute to parents or even throughout your grade level. Explain that published work needs to be error-free, so they will be using copy editor's symbols to lift each piece to "perfection"!

Cycles for Success With Capitalization

Rules for capitalization are important conventions. They signal readers and writers when words carry significance or when new sentences are beginning. In second and third grade, writers have often gained control over using capitals at the beginnings of sentences and in names. They are ready to branch out and explore a wider range of purposes for capitalization and to consider the way capitalized words are integrated into both their reading and their writing.

The Class Record-Keeping Grid: Capitalization on page 171 in the Assessment and Record Keeping section is especially helpful in monitoring your students' progress with capitalization. We encourage you to keep it handy as you circulate during writer's workshop or gather students for one-on-one conferences. With this tool in hand, you can quickly date the grid when you see evidence of a capitalization rule being followed or survey the grid to determine which students share a need for a capitalization review.

Cycles for Success With Capitalization

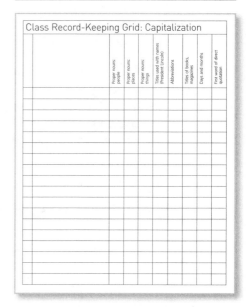

Capitalize for Emphasis

DAY 1   Model the Focus Point

When I want selected words to be read with great expression, I can capitalize all the letters. This tells my reader that these words need to be emphasized and read with gusto. The trick is to use this only once in a piece of writing. If you do it too much, the reader doesn't pay as much attention to your special word. I am writing a poem about breaking a vase. I want to start with *No! Stop!* I am going to use an exclamation point for *No* and *Stop*. I want to save my all-caps word for a bit later. My next two lines tell the reader what is happening. I don't think I am ready for an all-caps word yet; I am saving that for the climax. *CRASH* is my climax, the big moment when the vase explodes. Here is where I need those capital letters. Let's read this together with gusto!

> **Modeled Writing Sample**
>
> No! Stop!
>
> Eyes widen in horror
>
> Vase starts to rock
>
> CRASH
>
> Oops
>
> Sorry, Mom

 TURN AND TALK Writers, think about the ways I showed emphasis. What did you notice? Which word would you have chosen to capitalize?

 SUM IT UP To emphasize certain words, writers can capitalize all the letters in a word or use an interjection followed by an exclamation point.

DAY 2   Guided Practice

Place student writing on the overhead projector. Select the writing sample from page 180 or from your class that illustrates the use of all capitals in a word or interjections to show emphasis. If the author is one of your students, invite the author to read the selection to the class.

> **The Perfect Day**
> By Darrel T.
>
> Yesterday was a great day. It was snowing and snowing. It lasted all night and school was cancelled so my best friend and I built things in the snow ALL day long. There were snow people with faces and sticks for arms. They looked like marshmallow people. One time, we looked up and saw that the head had fallen off our snow boy. It rolled off and had landed with a big splat! We laughed and LAUGHED until we made strange noises with our noses. That made us laugh even More. My dog started barking and made a GRRRRR sound when we put the coats and hats on the snow people. He is pretty dumb sometimes. That made us start laughing all over again. Yesterday was a PERFECT day!

 TURN AND TALK Talk about the meaning of the writing; then, discuss a compliment you can offer the author. Think about using all capitals or interjections to show emphasis. Do you think these strategies were used too often, too little, or just right? Why?

If students have suggestions, receive author's permission before implementing changes.

 SUM IT UP Add "Capitalize for emphasis" to the class editing chart.

Remember, to show emphasis, writers can capitalize all the letters in a word or use an exclamation point to create an interjection.

DAY 3 Independent Practice

Walk writers through the process of selecting writing and then revisiting it for adding emphasis. Their goal is to reread to find places where they used or could use all capitals or insert an interjection to show emphasis.

PEER EDIT Take turns pointing out specific examples of using emphasis in your writing. Share your thinking about why you made those specific decisions.

SUM IT UP Writers can capitalize all the letters in a word or use an interjection followed by an exclamation point to show emphasis.

✅ Assess the Learning

- Have writers select a piece of writing that shows their aptitude at adding emphasis with capitalization and interjections. Meet with small groups and have them share their thinking as they selected words for emphasis.

- Meet with writers who are not independently using these strategies for adding emphasis. Assess their competency reading a selection from a book that includes capitalized words and/or exclamation points.

🔗 Link the Learning

- Have teams make a T-chart with one column labeled "ALL CAPS," the other "Interjections!" Students have five minutes to list words in each category. After time is called, have students take a gallery walk to view all the charts and consider the work of other teams.

- Have students select a page in their writer's notebook to label "Words to Show Emphasis." Their goal is to record capitalized words and interjections that might be used in their writing.

- Ask your media specialist or a bookstore to provide a list of picture books that use capitalization and interjections to show emphasis. Examples to consider: books by Mo Willems, such as *Don't Let the Pigeon Drive the Bus,* or David Shannon's *No, David!*

- Partners select a title with exclamation points and/or capitalized words to read to younger students *after* they become fluent (proper pacing, expression, phrasing, intonation, etc.) with the book and have practiced emphasizing key words.

Capitalize Proper Nouns: Persons, Places, and Things

DAY 1   Model the Focus Point

In today's writing I will focus on capitalizing the first letter in proper nouns. A proper noun names a specific person, place, or thing. Watch as I write some examples of proper nouns on this chart: _____ Elementary; the name of a business, such as Target; the name of a specific product, such as Crest toothpaste or Kleenex tissue; English muffin; American cheese. I am writing a poem about food. Watch as I write *Hershey bar*. Notice that I capitalize *Hershey* because that is the product name of the candy, but I don't capitalize *bar*. Next I will write *Butterfinger*. Should I capitalize this? I am going to add ice cream cone to my poem. Notice that I do not capitalize because this could be any kind of ice cream at all. If I said Baskin-Robbins ice cream, then I would need to capitalize *Baskin-Robbins* because that is the product name of a particular kind of ice cream.

> **Modeled Writing Sample**
>
> Hungry
>
> Hungry for a Hershey bar, Butterfinger too
>
> Hungry for an ice cream cone
>
> How about you?

TURN AND TALK Think about the words I capitalized and those that I didn't. Decide together why some specific words were capitalized and others were not.

SUM IT UP The names of particular people, places, or things need to be capitalized because they are all proper nouns.

DAY 2   Guided Practice

Place student writing on the overhead projector. Use the Interest Inventory writing sample from page 178, or one from your class that necessitates the capitalization of proper nouns. If the author is one of your students, invite the author to read the selection to the class.

TURN AND TALK Discuss the meaning of the piece and then give compliments about the writing. Think together about capitalizing the first letter of proper nouns.

Receive permission from the author before implementing changes.

SUM IT UP To your class editing chart, add "Capitalize proper nouns: Persons, places, and things."

Remember, writers capitalize the names of particular people, places, or things.

DAY 3 | **Independent Practice**

Thumb through a writing folder, showing writers how to select a sample that includes proper nouns. Model proofreading and editing for capitalization of proper nouns. Ask writers to select writing that includes proper nouns to proofread and edit for capitalization.

 PEER EDIT Share examples of proper nouns in your writing. Identify whether they are particular people, places, or things. If your writing included no proper nouns, working together, talk through ideas for adding them to your writing.

 SUM IT UP Always capitalize the first letter of nouns that name a particular person, place, or thing. These words are called proper nouns.

✅ Assess the Learning

- Use the Class Record-Keeping Grid: Capitalization, in the Assessment and Record Keeping section, page 171, to document students' use of capitalization of proper nouns.

- During writing conferences, have students identify proper nouns and explain their use.

∞ Link the Learning

- Read a variety of mentor books with proper nouns, such as *Wilfrid Gordon McDonald Partridge* by Mem Fox or *Chicken Sunday* by Patricia Polacco.

- See the Skills Continuum, Capitalization section, pages 34–35, for additional suggestions. Examples: titles used with names, Dr. Martin Luther King Jr.; abbreviations, Mr.; geographic names: planets (Earth), continents, countries, states, cities, landforms (Rocky Mountains); days and months; titles, *Time for Kids*; first word of direct quotation.

- Have students complete the Interest Inventory, from the Tools section, page 158. Remind them to pay attention to capitalizing proper nouns.

- Have students search for and circle proper nouns in newspapers and magazines.

Capitalize Titles and Headings

DAY 1 **Model the Focus Point**

Share several informational selections that have headings and titles.

> Today I am planning a nonfiction piece about the moons of Jupiter. As we saw, informational writing has a title and often several headings as well. To help me organize my writing, I am going to create some headings for a report. For my title I want to say, *Moonlight on Jupiter*. I will capitalize the first and last word and all other words that are important. That means I capitalize *Moonlight* and *Jupiter* for sure. I am not going to capitalize *on*. Help me think about capitalizing as I write out my headings. I am really wondering about the word *has* in Heading 2 and Heading 3. Help me think about that word and whether it should be capitalized. When I finish, I'll reread to check that my writing makes sense and double-check that I paid close attention to capitalizing for my titles and headings.

> **Modeled Writing Sample**
>
> Title: Moonlight on Jupiter
>
> Heading 1: Gazing at the Sky
>
> Heading 2: Earth Has One Moon
>
> Heading 3: Jupiter Has Sixty-Three Moons

TURN AND TALK Imagine that we get two new students and that you and your partner are responsible for explaining how to capitalize titles and headings. Decide what you would tell them.

SUM IT UP When writing titles and headings, use capitals for the first and last word and all other important words.

DAY 2 **Guided Practice**

Display a writing sample from your class that includes titles and headings, or the writing sample from page 188. If the author is one of your students, invite the author to read the selection to the class.

> **the dark**
>
> Some people fear the dark
>
> Darkness has the power to make you feel alone. Without light, your imagination can make you think that harmless things are suddenly scary.
>
> Things are different for nocturnal animals.
>
> Nocturnal animals love the dark because they can see very well. Their eyes are especially large and can reflect even small amounts of light back into the eye.

TURN AND TALK Share a compliment about the writing that you can offer the author. What can you say about the meaning of the selection? Think together about how the author used capitals in titles and headings. Tell each other the rule that applies.

Ask permission from the author before implementing changes.

SUM IT UP To a class editing chart, add "Capitalize the first and last word and other important words in titles and headings."

Remember, writers capitalize most words in titles or headings.

DAY 3 | **Independent Practice**

Prepare an informational passage that could have headings added and model proofreading for proper capitalization of titles and headings. Ask the writers to look in their folders and select writing that includes or could include a title and/or headings. Give them a few minutes to proofread and edit for capitalizations of these text features.

 PEER EDIT First, explain why you decided on the titles you wrote. Then, together, check over titles for correct capitalization. See if you have a place you could add some headings to help your reader know what might be coming next.

 SUM IT UP Capitalize the first, last, and all important words of titles and headings.

✓ Assess the Learning

- Review students' reading logs and writing folders for evidence of correct capitalization of titles.

- Review informational writing samples to check for capitalization in headings.

∞ Link the Learning

- Provide each student with a sticky note to record a read-aloud book recommendation. Include title, author, and year published. Cluster recommendations by title on the board. Select some titles for read-alouds. Challenge writers to correctly capitalize their titles.

- Have students complete a basic research report that includes the following: at least two resources, a title, a minimum of three sections with headings, a drawing with a caption, a labeled diagram, and a simple bibliography with titles, authors' names, and year published. Support correct use of capitalization.

- Have students review selected resources from science and social studies, examining capitalization of titles and headings, the table of contents, and index.

- Provide newspapers and have students discuss capitalization of titles, headlines, and headings in the newspaper. Point out that newspapers tend to have their own rules for capitalization and encourage conversations comparing capitalization in a newspaper with a magazine and a textbook.

Cycles for Improving Grammar Awareness

Read-alouds and the rich conversations we have with children all day long are essential building blocks of grammar development. Within the context of authors we love and the language we hear in our lives, our ear becomes tuned to what "sounds right." We come to expect certain sentence structures and notice when nouns and verbs do not agree. We notice when plurals are missing or tense is incorrect. When we *float learning on a sea of talk*, we maximize the potential for grammar and oral language development.

When focusing on grammar, take cues from your students. Listen to their oral language patterns and look closely at the grammar embedded within their writing samples. Pay special attention to English learners and to children who come from homes where nonstandard English is spoken. With careful attention to the language patterns that are already in place, you can direct their attention to the structures and forms woven into read-alouds, or extend and elaborate on what children say. For example, if a child says, *I goed to the store last night,* your response might be: *You went to the store! How lucky for you.* This elaboration and expansion of language supports and stretches learners.

Important Note: We must always respect home language and community culture, yet we have a responsibility to help learners understand and apply the more formal registers of English that are seen in published books and expected of proficient writers. While we would never show disrespect to native language patterns, we still need to help children learn that language shifts to match audience. For example, we can point out to our students that they use a different formal register when speaking to a principal or police officer than when they are conversing with friends or chatting with their families.

> **❝A word of caution: Some grammar programs teach rules in isolation. Research has shown this is a detached and futile exercise.❞**
> —*Donna Hooker Topping and Sandra Josephs Hoffman*

Complete Sentences vs. Fragments

DAY 1 — Model the Focus Point

Complete sentences have at least two parts, the *who or what did something* and *what they did*. In the sentence, *The mighty lion roars*, *lion* is the "what" and *roars* tells what the lion did. If I only write *The mighty lion* or only write *roars*, an important part of the sentence is missing. Those are sentence fragments, parts of sentences. In my second sentence, I want to tell how he walks in circles. What would happen if I said, *Walks in circles*? I will use our two important questions, *Who or what did something?* and *What did they do?* I am okay with what happened. I said *walks*. But the "who" is a problem. This is a fragment. Let's try again. How about *The king of the jungle walks in circles*.... Ask the two questions, *Who or what did something?* and *What did they do?* My last line is *The king of the jungle.* Check it with the two questions. Is it a sentence?

> ### Modeled Writing Sample
>
> The mighty lion roars, paces, and roars again. The king of the jungle walks in circles and then, with a sigh, arranges his huge body for sleep. The king of the jungle.

TURN AND TALK Think together. What are the two important questions we need to ask about every sentence we write? Are all of my sentences complete? Do I have any fragments?

SUM IT UP Remember, sentences require both the *who or what did something* and *what they did*. If either is missing, you need to add something to create a sentence.

DAY 2 — Guided Practice

Display student writing using a writing sample from the appendix, page 177 or from your class for students to examine together. If the author is your student, invite the author to read the selection to the class.

TURN AND TALK Talk about a celebration you can offer the author. Now, think about writing complete sentences. Tell each other the two essential components of a sentence. Then, determine if the author wrote complete sentences or sentence fragments by asking and answering, *Who or what did something?* or *What did they do?* Give suggestions for editing any fragments.

SUM IT UP To a class editing chart, add "Sentences = who/what did something + what they did."

To check for complete sentences ask the critical questions: *Who or what did something?* and *What did they do?*

Have students gather their writer's notebook and select a few pages to review. Display a poster with the sentence equation: "Sentence = *Who or what did something? + What did they do?*" Have students review the pages they have selected, challenging themselves to check every sentence on those pages for complete sentences.

PEER EDIT Working together, celebrate your complete sentences by telling your partner how you used the questions to check your sentences. Finally, select a sentence that you find interesting in each other's writing. Give reasons why you were drawn to that sentence.

SUM IT UP A complete sentence has two parts, the *who or what did something* and the part that tells *what they did*. If you have only one part, you have a fragment!

✔ Assess the Learning

- Provide writers with a collection of complete sentences and fragments. Have them sort the sentences and fragments into two piles. Identify those students who need additional support in recognizing complete sentences vs. fragments.

- During writing conferences, have writers assess some of their own sentences and demonstrate how they use the two critical questions.

∞ Link the Learning

- During silent reading, have students select a sentence or two to "test" with the two critical questions for sentence completeness. Have them record their selected sentences and findings to share after independent reading.

- Have students place sentences from favorite mentor texts on index cards. Create a class scramble by having students share their special sentence with a partner who then needs to answer the two critical questions.

- Gather those who are struggling to distinguish complete sentences from fragments into a guided writing experience where you can model and reteach this critical understanding.

- Have students review selections from their writer's notebook and writing folders to check for fragments, rewriting those that they discover.

- Use fragments to create a poem (see example at right) so students can see that fragments can be effectively used to build imagery in poetry. Good examples: *Dogsong* by Gary Paulsen or *Home Run* by Robert Burleigh.

> Big step up
> Noisy greeting
> Bus rolls on its way
> Chattering kids
> Stops and starts
> What a way to start the day

Sentence Parts: Subject and Verb

DAY 1 | **Model the Focus Point**

Note: Prepare a writing sample in advance.

A sentence has two basic parts, the subject and the verb. The subject is who or what the sentence is about. The verb is the second major part. It *often* says what the subject is doing, shows action. I have a T-chart labeled subject and verb. The answer to "Who or what did something?" identifies the subject. The answer to "What did they do?" identifies the verb. My second sentence is *We heard the sound. . . . We* is the subject and *heard* is the verb. My next sentence is *Sam and I stopped. . . . Sam and I* are both part of the subject. Think together. What is the verb? You aren't likely to make a chart like this for your writing, but it helps to think about subjects and verbs as you build your sentences into complete thoughts.

 TURN AND TALK Explain the two basic parts of sentences. Think of a new sentence that has both parts.

☺ **SUM IT UP** Answering these two questions, *Who or what did something?* and *What did they do?*, allows you to identify subject and verb. Remind each other, what a subject is and what a verb is?

Modeled Writing Sample

Cr-ee-ee-ee-k. We heard the sound in the darkness. Sam and I stopped cold. Neither of us moved a muscle. Then, without warning, the sound came again. Cr-ee-ee-ee-k. . . .

subject	verb
We	heard
Sam and I	stopped
Neither of us	moved
sound	came

DAY 2 | **Guided Practice**

Use the writing sample from page 187 or one from your class. Present copies to each pair of students or display on the overhead. If the author is one of your students, invite the author to read the selection to the class.

 TURN AND TALK Discuss the selection. Give the writer a compliment. Make a T-chart, labeling the left column *subject* and the right *verb*. Remember to ask *Who or what did something?* to identify the subject; then ask, *What did they do?* to identify the verb. Record your answers. If a subject or a verb is missing, write an *x*. We'll discuss your observations as a group.

☺ **SUM IT UP** To a class editing chart, add "Subject + verb = sentence."

Remember, sentences require two basic parts: the subject and the verb.

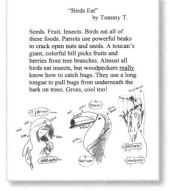

"Birds Eat"
by Tommy T.

Seeds. Fruit. Insects. Birds eat all of these foods. Parrots use powerful beaks to crack open nuts and seeds. A toucan's giant, colorful bill picks fruits and berries from tree branches. Almost all birds eat insects, but woodpeckers <u>really</u> know how to catch bugs. They use a long tongue to pull bugs from underneath the bark on trees. Gross, cool too!

DAY 3 | **Independent Practice**

Create a chart of key linking or helping verbs, including examples such as: *am, is, are, was,* and *were.* Remind students that these verbs don't show action, but they are still important verbs. Students will probably find linking or helping verbs in their writing. Model again how to identify the subject and verb. Have writers select a writing sample and begin to locate subjects and verbs in their own writing.

 PEER EDIT Explain to your thinking partner what you did to identify the subject and verb in your sentences. Share subject-verb examples from your own work.

 SUM IT UP To write a complete sentence, always include a subject, the *who or what did something* and the verb, *what they did.*

✅ Assess the Learning

- Meet with small groups of editors as they identify subjects and verbs to assess their ability to do so independently.

- Circulate during silent reading and ask each student to identify the subject and verb in sentences written by a mentor author.

🔗 Link the Learning

- Support students in working with the Create Your Own Resource: Identifying Verb Types from the Tools section, page 153. Model how to use the page by placing it on the overhead projector and showing writers how to complete it. Then, encourage them to work in partnerships to complete the form and install it in their writer's notebooks.

- Provide individual copies of a familiar shared reading passage. Have students circle the subjects and verbs. Share and compare.

- Provide photocopies of sentences and have students cut the sentences apart to separate the subject and the verb.

- Pull richly woven sentences from your favorite mentor texts. Place the sentences in a pocket chart and show the students how you can strip a sentence down to its base components, the subject and verb, and then rebuild the sentence back to its original rich state. Sentences with embedded clauses are particularly challenging for subject/verb identification and offer interesting extensions as students gain proficiency. A mentor text to consider is *Two Bad Ants* by Chris Van Allsburg.

Pronouns: Clarify Meaning

DAY 1 — Model the Focus Point

What if you heard the following: *He was really polite. He didn't act like a <u>really big star</u>*? Wouldn't you be thinking, *Come on! Tell us! Who are you talking about?* Well, sometimes writers forget to be clear about who or what they are describing. This leaves a reader feeling confused. When writers use pronouns like *he, she, it, we,* or *they,* it is important to check and be sure our reader knows who or what we are talking about. I am writing about the muscles of the heart. I want to start with *We are strong.* Oops. If I hadn't told you the topic, I bet you would already be wondering what I was talking about. I am going to change my beginning. What if I say, *We are the involuntary muscles of your heart. Strong and powerful, we beat every hour of every day.* Let's look at my pronouns. Did I make it clear to my reader what the *we* represents? Let's reread to check.

> **Modeled Writing Sample**
>
> We are the involuntary muscles of your heart. Strong and powerful, we beat every hour of every day.

 TURN AND TALK Think together. Identify the pronouns I used and be sure I made my thinking clear.

 SUM IT UP Writers must identify the noun, the who or what, that pronouns are referring to.

DAY 2 — Guided Practice

Provide a writing sample from the appendix, page 176, or from your class for students to review. If the author is one of your students, invite the author to read the selection to the class.

 TURN AND TALK Writers, talk about the content of the writing. Offer a specific compliment to the author. Reread each sentence, stopping to decide if you understand who or what is being described. Who or what the writing is about should always be clear to the reader.

 SUM IT UP To a class editing chart, add "Check pronouns so their meaning is clear."

DAY 3 | **Independent Practice**

Show writers how to look in their writing folders to select a piece of writing with pronouns and then to proofread and edit for pronoun usage. They need to check to ensure the "who or what" the writing is about is clear to the reader. Pronouns should clearly refer to their antecedents (the noun or pronoun). Give them a few minutes to proofread and edit away!

 PEER EDIT Take turns reading your writing and point out the pronouns you used and, even more important, where you named the noun or nouns they refer to.

 SUM IT UP A pronoun's job is to take the place of a noun. Use caution: Writers have a responsibility to be sure the *who* or *what* the writing is about is clear to a reader.

✓ Assess the Learning

- Provide partners with sentences such as: "He is my friend, but he moved away." "We went to the mall and got ice cream cones. We had a lot of fun." "Running and panting, with their paws digging into the snow, they ran on." Have partners cut the sentences up and then add words to clarify the pronoun. Assess to see who understands how to insert a noun or a name to add clarity.

- As you confer with individuals, ask them to show you places in their writing where they feel pronouns are clearly connected to antecedents.

∞ Link the Learning

- Select a mentor text, such as *When I Was Young in the Mountains* by Cynthia Rylant, and read it aloud, deliberately replacing all names with pronouns. Example: "When I was young in the mountains, he came home in the evening." Ask students to discuss what happens when pronouns are overused.

- Select a mentor text, such as *Sylvester and the Magic Pebble* by William Steig, and read a few pages aloud, deliberately replacing all pronouns with the names to which they refer. Ask the students to share their thinking about the impact on the story. Did they notice how repetitive and boring the overuse of names made the story?

- Have students select from their folders writing samples that have too many pronouns and rewrite them with a better balance between nouns and pronouns.

- Have students do a scavenger hunt for pronouns, collecting pronouns that are gender-specific, such as *he* and *she*, plural (*we* or *they*), and so on. Work together to create a class resource of pronouns that could be posted on the wall.

- Utilize Assessment Tool: Cloze for Pronoun Proficiency, on page 169. Have students fill in the blanks with nouns (no pronouns) and see how it sounds. Then have them proofread and edit for pronouns.

Pronoun Order: Person's Name and Then *I*, not *Me*

DAY 1   Model the Focus Point

When writing about someone else and you are in the story, too, there's a simple rule to follow: Write the other person's name first and then write *I*, instead of writing *me* as the subject of the sentence. I want to write about going fishing with my mom and dad when I was little. I will start by telling that my dad and I packed the car with our gear. I shouldn't say, *Me and my dad*, I should say, *My dad and I*. I'm being polite by using the other person's name first. Watch how I write *Mom* and then write *I* instead of *me*. *Mom and I carried the big basket of food*. I have to be careful. I can't say, *Me and Mom*. I need to say, *Mom and I*. When I'm finished, I'll proofread to check for *My dad and I*.

Modeled Writing Sample

Poles, Hooks and Worms: A Perfect Day

At daybreak, my dad and I stood at the car with poles, hooks, and worms ready to go. Mom and I carried the big basket of food to the car and we were off for our fishing adventure. As we drove out of town, my dad and I both knew that today was going to be a perfect day.

TURN AND TALK Think about my writing. Tell each other the rule to follow when writing about someone else when you're in the subject of the sentence, too.

SUM IT UP When you write about someone and you're in the story, too, write the other person's name first, then write *I*, instead of writing the word *me*. It's polite to do so.

DAY 2   Guided Practice

Display the writing sample from the appendix, page 185, or a selection from one of your students that includes a context for reviewing subjective noun-pronoun order. If the author is one of your students, invite the author to read the selection to the class.

Me and My Cousin

by Martha P.

Me and my cousins are very close. We even live on the same block and see each other every day. My favorite cousin is Jordon. She and me like to do a lot of the same things. We both like to make cookies. The whole house smells SO good. Her favorite cookie is chocolate chip. So is mine. Her favorite ice cream is chocolate-chocolate chip. So is mine. Her favorite candy is Hershey's chocolate bar, but I like M & M's. Oh, well. Two out of three is a lot in common!

TURN AND TALK Share things you appreciate about the writing. Proofread to check for noun-pronoun order. Did the author remember to be polite? What suggestions can you offer?

SUM IT UP To a class editing chart, add "In the subject of a sentence, write the other person's name, then *I*."

Always be polite and write or say the other person's name first.

DAY 3 | **Independent Practice**

Prepare a transparency of the Pronoun Order and Use page from the Assessment and Record Keeping section, page 175. Remind writers about the importance of following correct form. Ask the writers to select a writing sample from their folders where they wrote about someone else and they were in the story, too. Give them time to proofread and edit for "_____ and I."

 PEER EDIT Take turns showing each other where you wrote about someone else and you were in the story, too. Use a sticky note to mark the page each time you wrote the other person's name, and then wrote *I*, not *me*. Think together about your writing.

SUM IT UP When we are speaking and when we are writing, we need to be polite and state another person's name first before saying *I*.

✔ Assess the Learning

- Assess writers' understanding of subjective noun-pronoun order by having students complete the Pronoun Order and Use page. Collect and record scores. Analyze error patterns to inform your instruction.

- Have individual students orally generate sentences that demonstrate correct subjective noun-pronoun order

🔗 Link the Learning

- Pull together guided writing groups of students who had difficulty using the Pronoun Order and Use sheet. Reteach the key points and have them practice the idea again in their writing.

- Have teams create correct and incorrect examples of subjective noun-pronoun order on transparencies. Share their examples with the class.

- Encourage students to tell about events in their lives using the correct subjective noun-pronoun order to describe the events.

- Try applying the rule to three people: "My mother, my father, and I…."

Single vs. Double Subjects
(*My mom* vs. *My mom she*)

DAY 1 — Model the Focus Point

The subject is the part of the sentence that tells who or what is doing something. A tricky rule we need to learn is that we can only tell who a sentence is about one time in each sentence. I want to say: *Abraham Lincoln was our 16th president*. I would not say, *Abraham Lincoln, he was our 16th president* because Abraham Lincoln and *he* are the same person. That would be telling who the sentence is about twice!! My second sentence is about his wife, Mary. I will be very careful to avoid saying *Mary, she* because I don't want to double up! Finally, I'll reread to see if my writing makes sense and then I'll check the sentence to make sure I didn't tell who the sentence is about more than once.

> **Modeled Writing Sample**
>
> Abraham Lincoln was our 16th president. His wife, Mary, was frequently ill, so she did not travel with him very often. Abraham Lincoln was famous for his kindness and honesty. He was a president I would like to have known as a friend.

 TURN AND TALK Talk about what I was careful <u>not</u> to do with the subject of my sentences.

SUM IT UP Remember, when you write about someone or something, use either the subject's name or a pronoun for the name in the same sentence. Don't use both the name and the pronoun in one sentence. That's doubling up!

DAY 2 — Guided Practice

Prepare the writing sample from page 186 in the appendix or a selection from one of your students that includes an opportunity to talk about the dangers of doubling the subject. If the author is one of your students, invite the author to read the selection to the class.

> **Bird Watching Field Trip**
>
> Last weekend my family we went bird watching. I thought it was going to be boring and didn't want to go. My parents they told me that we were going as a family and we were going to have fun whether I liked it or not. They smiled at me and I frowned at them. To make a long story short we had an ok time. We saw hawks, swallows, and some really cool flicker. I used binoculars for the first time, got to walk across a stream on slippery rocks, and got ice cream on the way home. I guess sometimes parents they make good plans.

 TURN AND TALK Writers, talk about the writing, then offer a specific compliment about something the writer did well. Go back and reread each sentence and identify the subject. Then check to see if the author doubled up on the subject by saying, for example, *Last weekend my family we*

SUM IT UP To the class editing chart, add "Use a noun or a pronoun to name your subject. Not both!"

Remember, use the subject name only once in a sentence.

Guide writers in selecting a different piece of writing, and then show how to proofread and edit for doubling up on the subject. Give them a few minutes to put on their editors' caps to check their own writing.

 PEER EDIT Take turns pointing out the subject of each of your sentences. Together, carefully proofread each paper for any double subjects.

 SUM IT UP Remember, when writing about someone or something, use the subject's name or a pronoun for the name. Don't use both!

✓ Assess the Learning

- Observe editors at work. Use a class record-keeping grid to note both orally and in writing which students are still doubling up subjects in the sentences.

- Use the Double Subjects resource, on page 174, to assess understanding.

Link the Learning

- During writer's workshop remind students about not doubling up the subject. Help writers apply what they know as they craft writing selections.

- Teach a cycle about compound subjects (Ex: "Mom and dad…"), demonstrating that compound subjects are correct, while double subjects such as "My mom, she. . ." are incorrect.

- Deliberately slip double subjects into your conversation with students, then pause and wait for them to notice. Have partners then restate the sentence in the correct form.

- Have each student identify a favorite book in which the central character names him or herself along with another person in a sentence. Notice how the author constructs these sentences. Examples: *When I Was Young in the Mountains* by Cynthia Rylant; *A Chair for My Mother* by Vera B. Williams; *The Ghost-Eye Tree* by Bill Martin Jr. and John Archambault; and *Owl Moon* by Jane Yolen.

Singular Subject-Verb Agreement

DAY 1 | **Model the Focus Point**

When we write sentences about a singular subject, our verb has to match. I am writing about a baby sea turtle. Because I am writing about one turtle, I need to be careful with the verbs I choose to make sure they work with a singular subject. My first sentence is *A baby sea turtle hatches.* . . . I want to look closely at the verb to be sure it agrees. Should it say *hatch* or *hatches*? *A baby sea turtle hatch* doesn't sound right to me. I need the *s* on *hatches*. My next sentence is *The baby digs and digs.* . . . I need to check the verb. I still have a single baby turtle. Should the verb be *dig* or *digs*? It should definitely be *digs*. If I were writing about turtles, then I could use *dig*. Since this is singular, one baby, I need to say *digs*. Did you notice how both verbs, *hatches* and *digs*, needed an *s* to agree with the singular subject?

> **Modeled Writing Sample**
>
> Baby Sea Turtles
>
> A baby sea turtle hatches out of its egg, alone with no mother in sight. The baby digs and digs, using its tiny little legs to move through the sand and up to the surface.

TURN AND TALK Remember, my subject is one single turtle. Verbs that you will often see with singular subjects include *is*, *was*, *has*, and action verbs ending in *s*. Think together. If I were to add another sentence, what could I write? Careful with the verb. Be sure it matches a singular subject.

SUM IT UP When writing about a singular subject, you will usually use the verbs *is*, *was*, or action words ending in *s*.

DAY 2 | **Guided Practice**

Use the writing sample from the appendix, page 177, or a sample from your class that invites singular subject-verb agreement. If the author is one of your students, invite the author to read the selection to the class.

TURN AND TALK Note: Partners will need a blank piece of paper and pencil.

First, talk over the meaning of the selection and share a compliment about the writing. Now, make and label a T-chart that says "subject" on one side and "verb" on the other. Find and write the subject and verb in each sentence. Put a star next to the subjects that are singular and pay attention to the verbs to be sure they match.

SUM IT UP To a class editing chart, add "Singular subjects need a verb that matches."

Remember, when your sentence has a singular noun, the sentence needs a verb that agrees.

DAY 3 | **Independent Practice**

Model how to look for subject-verb agreement in a piece of writing selected from a writing folder. Give writers a few minutes to check their papers to search for a singular subject and to check the verb. Remind them that singular verbs may include *is*, *was*, *has*, and action verbs ending in *s*.

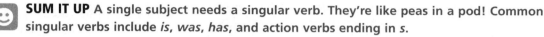 **PEER EDIT** Put your heads together and find singular subjects and verbs. Did you find sentences with *is*, *was*, *has*, or action verbs that end in *s*? Share those sentences.

SUM IT UP A single subject needs a singular verb. They're like peas in a pod! Common singular verbs include *is*, *was*, *has*, and action verbs ending in *s*.

✔ Assess the Learning

- Use a class record-keeping grid as you observe editors at work. Check off the students who write singular subject–verb agreements correctly.

- Confer one on one, asking writers to point out singular subjects and verbs in their writing or reading materials.

∞ Link the Learning

- Gather students who need additional support with subject-verb agreement into a small-group guided writing experience.

- Play a singular-plural noun game. You say a plural noun and the students need to give its singular form or vice versa, then create a sentence with a verb that matches. Example: Teacher says, "Turtles." Students say "turtle" and then "A turtle digs holes in the sand."

- Use math books to find story problems and identify whether they include singular nouns and verbs.

- Read favorite books and copy selected sentences with singular subjects and verbs onto chart paper or strips for a pocket chart. Examples: In *Chicken Little* by Steven Kellogg, "The sky is falling!" "Henny Penny was horrified." In *Chicken Sunday* by Patricia Polacco, "That Easter bonnet in Mr. Kodinski's window is the most beautiful I ever did see. . . ." Change these sentences from singular to plural.

Plural Subject-Verb Agreement

DAY 1 **Model the Focus Point**

Note: Use the modeled writing sample from the Singular Subject-Verb Agreement cycle.

> **Modeled Writing Sample**
>
> Baby Sea Turtles
>
> A baby sea turtle hatches out of its egg, alone with no mother in sight. The baby digs and digs, using its tiny little legs to move through the sand and up to the surface.

When sentences have a plural subject, meaning more than one, then the verb has to agree. Here's an example: *Our bikes <u>are</u> cool!* But *Our bikes <u>is</u> cool!* does not work. I am going to work on a piece of writing I did about one baby turtle, but now I am going to switch from singular, one baby turtle, to plural, and write about *turtles.* As you know, that means I will need to check my verbs very carefully. *Baby sea turtle(s)....* I have taken out *A* and added an *s* to make *turtle* plural—now let's look at the verb. *Baby sea turtles hatches....* Oooops. The verb doesn't work. I need to remove the /es/ to make the verb agree with the new plural subject. My next sentence needs to say *babies* instead of *baby.* Let's look at the verb and decide what to do. I want to add one more sentence, *They have to work hard....* Should I choose *have* or *has* to go with the subject, *they*?

 TURN AND TALK What have you noticed about working with plural subjects and making verbs agree or match? Discuss the ways to know that a subject is plural. We will make a chart of plural subjects and some verbs that agree or match.

 SUM IT UP When writing about two or more people, places, or things, write their proper names or the word *they.* Then, use the verbs *are, were, have,* or plural action verbs.

DAY 2 **Guided Practice**

Display the writing sample from page 187 or a sample from your class. If the author is one of your students, invite the author to read the selection to the class.

"Birds Eat"
by Tommy T.

Seeds. Fruit. Insects. Birds eat all of these foods. Parrots use powerful beaks to crack open nuts and seeds. A toucan's giant, colorful bill picks fruits and berries from tree branches. Almost all birds eat insects, but woodpeckers <u>really</u> know how to catch bugs. They use a long tongue to pull bugs from underneath the bark on trees. Gross, cool too!

TURN AND TALK Talk about the meaning of the selection and give a compliment about the writing. Read the selection and talk about the verbs. Discuss: If you changed this to singular subjects, what verbs would you use?

SUM IT UP To a class editing chart, add "Plural subjects need plural verbs."

Remember, when your sentence has a plural subject, the sentence also needs a plural verb.

DAY 3 | **Independent Practice**

Scan a writing folder for a sample with plural subjects. Have students listen as you think aloud, proofreading for plural subject-verb agreement. Turn the proofreading and editing process over to the students as they search their own work.

 PEER EDIT Together proofread one writing selection from each of your folders or notebooks, pointing out the plural subjects and verbs.

 SUM IT UP A plural subject needs a plural verb. They're like two peas in a pod!

✓ Assess the Learning

- Use a class record-keeping grid as you observe editors. Check off the students who write plural subject–verb agreements correctly.

- Confer with readers during independent reading and have them identify singular and plural subjects and verbs in their selections.

Link the Learning

- Read Doreen Cronin's wonderful *Click, Clack Moo: Cows That Type* to search for the mix of singular and plural subjects and their matching verbs.

- Have students create a Concentration game by placing singular and plural subjects and verbs on cards and then trying to create matches.

- Read *Animals Nobody Loves* by Seymour Simon. Help students notice that the subjects of some sections are singular and others are plural. Keep a chart of the verbs Seymour Simon matches to the subjects.

- Give students wipe-off boards. Say a verb. Have students write it, identify the verb as singular or plural, and then add a suitable subject.

Adjectives to Lift Descriptions

DAY 1   **Model the Focus Point**

Read aloud from *Amos & Boris* by William Steig, the page that begins, "One night, in a phosphorescent sea…" and deliberately leave out the adjectives. Then read it again, with the adjectives in place.

> **Can you believe the difference it made when those marvelous describing words were removed? Adding strong adjectives, words that describe nouns and pronouns, helps readers to visualize. As a writer, I need to collect stellar adjectives so I can use them in my writing. I am going to write some words from this book in my writer's notebook. *Luminous* is my first entry. I love that word. I think of luminous water, luminous sky, Aricelli's luminous eyes. I also want to save the word *immense*. That is so much richer than just *big*. I will add *immense* to my list. I love collecting these words! Let's reread what I have so far. I know you are going to want to start a section in your writer's notebook with stellar adjectives.**

> **TURN AND TALK** Keep thinking about my list of adjectives. Which words on my list would you want on a list of stellar adjectives? Select a marvelous adjective you want to add to your adjective list!

> **SUM IT UP** Adjectives are words that describe nouns and pronouns. Writers need to go "beyond the basics" and use stellar adjectives.

Modeled Writing Sample	
Stellar Adjectives	
luminous	healthy
immense	huge
exquisite	short-cropped hair
exceptional	honest
unusual	awesome

DAY 2   **Guided Practice**

Display a piece of writing that has stellar adjectives or could benefit from having some. Use the writing sample from page 185, or a sample from your class. If the author is one of your students, have the author read the selection to the class.

> **TURN AND TALK** Read together and come up with a compliment for the author. Reread each sentence, checking for adjectives. When you find one, decide if the writer was a risk taker and chose adjectives that went *beyond the basics*. When you find a stellar adjective, imagine that the author is sitting with you and whisper, *Way to go, writer!*

> **SUM IT UP** To a class editing chart, add "Choose stellar adjectives!"

> Include carefully selected describing words in your writing. Writers who are ready may add this to a personal log of editing tips.

> A walrus went swiming in the Ocean one day he jumt in the water and all fish swan away his tusks were sharp and long and white. they no he can eat them all in One bite.

Have writers review their writer's notebook and select one example that they want to enrich with stellar adjectives. Post the "Stellar Adjectives" list from the modeled writing earlier in this cycle. Give writers time to reread, add adjectives, and get ready to share with a partner.

 PEER EDIT Take turns reading your writing and pointing out adjectives. Evaluate your own adjectives. Together, brainstorm adjectives that you could help each other add. Look at the section of your writer's notebook where you are collecting stellar adjectives. Which favorite mentor books will you use to try to add to your list?

 SUM IT UP Remember, well-chosen adjectives are like jewels. They make our writing sparkle!

✓ Assess the Learning

- Analyze students' writing for well-selected adjectives. On a class record-keeping grid note writers who are "adjective risk takers" and those who need more coaching.

- During independent reading, confer with individuals to assess their ability to recognize adjectives and to record personal favorites in their writer's notebook to use later in their own writing.

Link the Learning

- Highlight picture books with exquisite language, particularly adjectives. *Sylvester and the Magic Pebble, Amos and Boris,* or *Shrek,* by William Steig; *Some Smug Slug* by Pamela Duncan Edward; and *Lilly's Purple Plastic Purse* by Kevin Henkes are among our favorites. You might also enjoy *Many Luscious Lollipops* by Ruth Heller or the beautifully crafted *My Mama Had a Dancing Heart* by Libba Moore Gray. Share your beloved books and the language they inspire.

- Record tantalizing words from read-alouds. Make a conscious effort to use these adjectives from the chart in writing and in daily conversation. Challenge your students to use them in daily conversation and in writing.

- Have students use The Parts of Speech, in the Tools section, page 155, to record adjectives—not random adjectives, but stellar, personal favorites. Have them place this tool in their writer's notebook for future reference as they craft beautiful language.

Adjectives: Comparative and Superlative Forms

DAY 1 | Model the Focus Point

I have asked three students of three different heights to line up from shortest to tallest. Listen as I describe them. Tiana is tall. Morgan is tall<u>er</u>. Ali is the tall<u>est</u>. Did you notice the way I changed the word *tall* as I compared their heights? Here is another way to compare. Ali is energetic. Tiana is a bit <u>more</u> energetic. Morgan is the <u>most</u> energetic of all. We can also use *more* and *most* to support our comparisons. I am writing about the greatest clean-up team ever. They are better than great. They are better than greater. They are the great<u>est</u>. I think it would be a good idea to thank the custodian. Watch as I write her a letter.

 TURN AND TALK What did you notice about my comparisons? Use your wipe-off boards and write down the comparison words I used in this letter. Think together about comparisons you can make using *big, bigger, biggest; small, smaller, smallest; loud, louder, loudest.* Think of comparisons using more and most!

SUM IT UP We can compare nouns or pronouns using *-er* and *-est* or *more* and *most*. Be aware of multisyllable words, which often use *more* and *most* in comparison.

> **Modeled Writing Sample**
>
> Date _____
>
> Dear _____,
>
> Thank you for organizing the *greatest* student clean-up team ever. Previous clean-up teams have worked *hard*. This team worked *harder* than ever and was the *most* organized team we've ever encountered. Hats off to the *hardest* working clean-up crew! Thank you.
>
> Sincerely,

DAY 2 | Guided Practice

Display this writing sample from appendix page 181 or one from a student author in your class. If the author is one of your students, have the author read the selection to the class.

 TURN AND TALK Discuss the writing's meaning and offer a compliment to the author. Reread the selection with the idea of inserting comparisons using *-er*, *-est*, *more*, and *most* to show comparisons.

SUM IT UP To a class editing chart, add "To show comparisons, use *-er*, *-est*, *more*, or *most* with adjectives."

> June 4th
>
> The best day of the year is when I get to see my grandma and grandpa. They are always excited to see ME! They live way far away in Peru. It takes us forever! First there is the plane. Then there is a bus full of people on bumpy roads. Forever!! Forever!! Forever!! But it is all worth it because they love ME! I love them so much. Don't you LOVE Grandparents?

Model how to reread a piece of writing to notice or insert comparative and superlative adjectives. Give writers time to rethink and insert adverbs or adjectives that compare.

 PEER EDIT Work together to find examples in your writing folders where you can add adjectives that compare. Check for *-er* and *-est* endings, as well as *more* and *most*.

 SUM IT UP Use comparative forms. Pay attention to the way you form adjectives using *-er* and *-est* endings, *more*, and *most*.

✔ Assess the Learning

- Confer with writers and ask them to use a variety of forms to compare real things in the classroom. Identify those who can compare using regular forms and those who are ready for irregular or special comparatives. See the table below in Link the Learning.

- Have students create a page in their writer's notebook where they collect and save comparative adjectives they find in their reading and in their own writing. Gather the notebooks and assess the comparatives they collected.

Link the Learning

- Place the first sentence of *Shrek* by William Steig in a pocket chart. "His mother was ugly and his father was ugly, but Shrek was uglier than the two of them put together." Guide students in a conversation about the imagery generated by the comparatives and then have partners generate similar sentences of their own to display in the chart.

- Teach terms associated with these forms: comparatives compare two nouns/pronouns; superlatives compare three or more nouns or pronouns.

- Some adjectives use completely different words to show comparison. Provide your students with opportunities to use a broad range of language forms that show comparison.

	Comparative	Superlative
bad	worse	worst
good	better	best
many	more	most

- Notice how spelling changes in some comparatives: With consonant-y patterns, change the *y* to *i* and add the ending (*funny, funnier, funniest; happy, happier, happiest*). Have students conduct a scavenger hunt for comparatives that are regular and those that require a special rule.

Adverbs and Adverb Phrases as Sentence Openers

DAY 1 — Model the Focus Point

Adverbs and adverb phrases (which are also called prepositional phrases) tell where, when, how, and to what extent something happens. These are powerful tools that lift our writing and pull readers right into the setting. I want my reader to join me on the edge of a cliff, so I will use an adverb phrase after an opener that's followed by a comma to begin. *At the stroke of midnight, Inez crept slowly along the edge of the cliff. . . "* Close your eyes and visualize. Are you on the cliff, in the dark? Watch as I underline the adverb phrase I used. In sentence two, I will open with another adverb, but this time I will use a single adverb, *quickly*. Notice how I place a comma after *quickly*. When we open with an adverb or an adverb phrase, we often use a comma before writing the rest of the sentence. Think together about my sentences and the way I opened with an adverb or emphasized an adverb phrase. I love the way adverbs add energy and sensory images to our writing!

> **Modeled Writing Sample**
>
> At the stroke of midnight, Inez crept slowly along the edge of the cliff. Quickly, she looked back to see if anyone was following.

 TURN AND TALK Post a chart of the adverbs listed in the Tools section, page 154, to assist the students.

Adverbs and adverb phrases tell how, when, or where. Single adverbs work with verbs to add clarity and meaning, as in *walk slowly*. Slowly tells <u>how</u> someone walked. Notice the *-ly*. That is often a signal for an adverb. I underlined some of the adverbs and adverb phrases but there are more. See if you can find them.

 SUM IT UP Adverbs and adverb phrases answer the questions how, where, when, and to what extent something was done. Adverbs usually end in *-ly*.

DAY 2 — Guided Practice

Display the writing sample from page 186, or a sample from your class. If the author is one of your students, invite the author to read the selection to the class.

> **Racoon**
>
> While we sleep, he trundles on light feet confident and sure. Quietly, his shadow moves through the darkness, searching. Within the misty night, his masked face and glowing eyes keep careful watch for predator and prey. Shhh! He pauses. _____
>
> _____

 TURN AND TALK Discuss the content of the writing and prepare a compliment for the author. Notice the adverbs and adverb phrases that open the sentences. How do the adverbs add strength to this writing? What can you learn from this writer?

 SUM IT UP To a class editing chart, add "Adverbs and adverb phrases are great sentence openers."

Help writers search their notebooks and writing folders for places where they can enhance sentence openings with adverbs and adverb phrases. Give them a few minutes to proofread and edit away!

 PEER EDIT Take turns reading your writing and point out places where you used adverbs and adverb phrases as sentence openers. Show how you used a comma after the opener. Use sticky notes to identify single adverbs that end in *-ly*.

 SUM IT UP Adverbs and adverb phrases make powerful sentence openers. Use these tools to bring your reader right into your setting, but remember to follow them with a comma, except for short adverb phrases!

 Assess the Learning

- Survey writing samples to assess students' understanding of how to craft an opener using an adverb or adverb phrase.

- Observe writers at work and look for evidence of adverbs or have students identify adverbs and adverb phrases in their reading selections.

Link the Learning

- Have fun with adverbs in *Dearly, Nearly, Insincerely: What Is An Adverb?* by Brian Cleary and *Up, Up and Away: A Book About Adverbs* by Ruth Heller.

- Read *Annie and the Old One* by Miska Miles to observe how the author uses adverbial phrases to show passage of time, or *Dogsong* by Gary Paulsen to explore how opening with adverb phrases enhances the rich settings.

- Provide students with Create Your Own Resource: Understanding Adverbs and Prepositional Phrases, page 154, and have them complete it to add it to their writer's notebook.

- Adverbs often end in *-ly*. Have writers think together and make a list of *-ly* words to keep in their writer's notebook. Exceptions to the typical rules of adverbs include: *not, never, very,* and *always*.

Verbs: Linking and Helping

DAY 1 **Model the Focus Point**

We know about the importance of strong action verbs, the engines of our sentences. But there are two other important kinds of verbs that we use in our writing: linking verbs and helping verbs. These verbs do not show action. I am writing about George Washington's teeth. My first sentence is *George Washington was our. . . .* The verb is *was*. That is a linking verb. It links George to the word *president*. I will draw a line under that linking verb. In the second sentence, *Some people were saying. . . ,* *saying* is the action verb, isn't it? But we also have a helping verb, *were*. The two work together. Let's draw a line under that, too. Help me watch for linking verbs and helping verbs. When I'm finished, I'll reread to check my verbs.

> **Modeled Writing Sample**
>
> **Poor George**
>
> George Washington was our first president. Some people were saying that he wore wooden teeth. Those people were incorrect. All but two of his teeth had fallen out so he had false teeth made from metal and bone.

TURN AND TALK Note: Provide partners with wipe-off boards or paper.

Writers, focus on the verbs. I used three kinds of verbs today. Think together and write the verbs I used. What kind of verbs are you writing?

SUM IT UP Writers use three types of verbs: action, linking, and helping verbs.

DAY 2 **Guided Practice**

Display a writing selection that includes linking and helping verbs. Use the writing sample from page 180, or one from your class. If the author is one of your students, invite the author to read the selection to the class. It will be helpful to post a chart listing examples of action, linking, and helping verbs. (See Tools, page 153, for ideas.)

> **The Perfect Day**
> By Darrel T.
>
> Yesterday was a great day. It was snowing and snowing. It lasted all night and school was cancelled so my best friend and I built things in the snow ALL day long. There were snow people with faces and sticks for arms. They looked like marshmallow people. One time, we looked up and saw that the head had fallen off our snow boy. It rolled off and had landed with a big splat! We laughed and LAUGHED until we made strange noises with our noses. That made us laugh even More. My dog started barking and made a GRRRRR sound when we put the coats and hats on the snow people. He is pretty dumb sometimes. That made us start laughing all over again. Yesterday was a PERFECT day!

TURN AND TALK Discuss the writing. Prepare a compliment for the author. Now, think about the three types of verbs: action, linking, and helping verbs. Decide which linking or helping verbs the author used or could have used.

SUM IT UP Create a class verb chart with three columns.

There are three types of verbs that we need to use in our writing: action, linking, and helping. For the next few days, collect your favorite examples of each type and we will add them to our class verb chart.

Refer to the chart of verb types. Select a sample from a student writing folder and model proofreading for types of verbs. Refer to the posted verb types during your think–aloud. Turn the responsibility over to the students to review their writing for examples of linking and helping verbs.

 PEER EDIT Show your writing to your partner. Show places where you have used different kinds of verbs in your writing.

 SUM IT UP Verbs are important parts of speech. They can show action (*run*). They can link or connect the subject (George Washington) with words (*our first president*) after the linking verb (*was*). They can also help other verbs (*were saying*).

✓ Assess the Learning

- Use the Create Your Own Resource: Identifying Verb Types resource in the Tools section, page 153, to assess student understanding. You may want to have students complete the tool in small groups so you can closely observe and assess their learning.

- During writing conferences, have students explain the function of a linking verb and a helping verb.

Link the Learning

- Have students complete the Create Your Own Resource: Identifying Verb Types and insert it into their writer's notebook as an ongoing reference.

- Read Ruth Heller's *Kites Sail High: A Book About Verbs*, stopping for partner discussion of verbs.

- Read *Tomorrow's Alphabet* by George Shannon for a great experience with linking verbs.

- *The Librarian of Basra* by Jeanette Winter weaves helping verbs throughout this fascinating, true story.

- Provide students with copies of a passage, such as the George Washington sample in this cycle. Have them use scissors to remove the verbs and verb phrases and then sort them into categories for action, linking, or verb phrases. Repeat the experience with a passage from a familiar picture book.

Verbs: Present and Past Tenses

DAY 1 | Model the Focus Point

When writers want to show that something is happening in the present or in the past, they make changes to verbs. If we were to say, *We snap our fingers.* That would mean we are snapping "right now." If we say, *We snapp<u>ed</u> our fingers*, that would mean we already did it! I am writing a book review about *Animals Nobody Loves* by Seymour Simon. I already read the book, so I will be writing using past-tense verbs. I want to say, *We learned about. . . .* I could say we *learn* but that means right now. I need to add the *-ed* ending so this is past tense. Next, I want to tell how Seymour Simon described the animals. I need to be careful and add that *-ed* ending. When I am finished writing, I will reread carefully and check these verbs one last time.

> **Modeled Writing Sample**
>
> Book Review
>
> In *Animals Nobody Loves*, we learned about all sorts of amazing animals. Seymour Simon described animals that have big feet, strange habits, or poisonous venom. I hated to put it down!

TURN AND TALK Focus on the verbs. I wrote this piece in the past tense. How can you tell? Challenge yourself to change the verbs to present tense.

SUM IT UP Verbs can help writers show present or past tense.

DAY 2 | Guided Practice

Display a writing sample. You may want to select Head Lice from page 188 or a sample from your class. If the author is one of your students, invite the author to read the selection to the class.

TURN AND TALK Discuss the writing's meaning. Share a compliment about it. Now, think about the verbs. Are they in the present or past tense? Give examples from the writing.

SUM IT UP To a class editing chart, add "Adjust verbs to show present or past tense."

Verb tenses change according to the time when the action occurs.

> Head Lice
>
> I have this teacher. She is really nice. But some time I think she has head lice. She itches all day. And the last time for head lice check She got sent home from school. I want tell you more but it is not cool. The day she came back she had no hair and her head was bear. I think to my self how did she get the lice. I kept on thinking until I new that I was not nice because I'm the one who gave her the lice.
>
> By: Samantha

DAY 3 | **Independent Practice**

Select a sample from a student writing folder and model proofreading for verb tenses. First read it as it is, then "try on" verbs of different tenses. Turn the responsibility over to the students as they shift to reviewing their own writing folders.

 PEER EDIT Show your writing to your partner. Point out your verbs and talk about what tenses you have used. Next, change the tense of a few verbs and see how it sounds. Does the change match the rest of the piece? Once you start in a certain tense, you should stick to it, unless you are deliberately adding a flashback.

SUM IT UP Verb tenses help readers know if the action is taking place in the present or in the past.

✔ Assess the Learning

- Use a Class Record-Keeping Grid on page 170 to collect data on your students' use of present- and past-tense verbs in their writing folders.

- Use Assessment Tool: Cloze for Verb Tenses (page 168) during a small-group, partner, or independent experience. Select appropriate tenses according to your students' level of understanding.

∞ Link the Learning

- Note: In present tense we add *-s* or *-es* to verbs when matching to the *he/she/it* subject (third-person singular).

- Read sentences aloud, providing examples of different tenses. Determine which students can identify the tense and/or change the verb from one tense to another.

- Introduce the future tense, supported with helping verbs: *will, shall, hope to*, and so on. Create a modeled writing lesson emphasizing future tense.

- Create two charts to keep ongoing collections of regular verbs (made past tense by adding *-ed* or when using helping verbs *has, have, had*) and irregular verb constructions, such as: *go/went*; *has/have/had gone*; *write/wrote/written*; *do/did/done*. Have students collect words from favorite books to add to the chart.

- Read *Alexander and the Terrible, Horrible, No Good, Very Bad Day* by Judith Viorst and check out the verbs.

Cycles for Lifting Punctuation

Well-designed punctuation controls the flow of a message, helps the reader understand nuances of meaning, and makes the texts more interesting! Punctuation should not be limited to end-of-process corrections; rather, we believe it should be recast as a tool we use to shape our thoughts. Our objective is to support writers in understanding that punctuation, when thoughtfully used, can lift the quality of our writing. With this in mind, we coach writers to think about punctuation at two significant points in the writing process:

1. During drafting: Here punctuation turns our thinking toward interesting phrasing, addition of onomatopoeia and sound words, stimulating emotion in the reader with exclamation marks, creating an interesting opener to follow with a comma, and so on.

2. During editing: This is where we reread for the proper use of conventions to ensure that we have applied punctuation that will help a reader navigate our work.

Above all, we focus on transferring knowledge of punctuation across a wide variety of contexts so that writers generalize their knowledge and can apply appropriate punctuation across all texts.

End Punctuation: Period, Question Mark, and Exclamation Point

DAY 1 Model the Focus Point

There are three kinds of punctuation we use at the end of sentences: a period, a question mark, or an exclamation point. Turn and tell a partner why you use each one. As writers, we need to think about using all three kinds of sentences to make our writing interesting to our readers. I am writing about having a really bad day. For my title I will say, *Could It Get Worse?* Did you notice I created a question for the title? Writers do that sometimes. My first sentence, *What a day I've had!*, ends with an exclamation point to give it emphasis. So far I have a question and an exclamatory sentence. Now, I need a plain old declarative sentence with a period. As soon as I've finished writing for today, I'll proofread, or recheck to make certain that I used the correct end punctuation.

> **Modeled Writing Sample**
>
> Could It Get Worse?
>
> What a day I've had! On my way to work, my car ran out of gas. Then, I had to walk to the gas station. Once I reached the station, my feet were killing me, my spirits were low, and I was late for work. Could anything else go wrong?
>
> Written and lived by_____

TURN AND TALK Writers, check out the different punctuation marks I used. How did they add to my writing? Reread my writing without the exclamation or question marks.

SUM IT UP Remember, using different end punctuation marks for different kinds of sentences adds depth and interest to our writing.

DAY 2 Guided Practice

Place a piece of writing on the overhead projector. Use the writing sample from page 181 or a writing sample from your class. If the author is one of your students, invite the author to read the selection to the class.

TURN AND TALK What can you say about the meaning of the selection? Offer a compliment to the author. Decide if the writer effectively used different end punctuation marks for different kinds of sentences. Are there any places where the punctuation should be different? Could you create a title that is a question?

SUM IT UP To a class editing chart, add "Use a variety of end punctuation (?.!)."

Writers use different end punctuation marks for declarative, exclamatory, and interrogative sentences.

> June 4th
>
> The best day of the year is when I get to see my grandma and grandpa. They are always excited to see ME! They live way far away in Peru. It takes us forever! First there is the plane. Then there is a bus full of pople on bumpy roads. Forever!! Forever!! Forever!! But it is all worth it because they love ME! I love them so much. Don't you LOVE Grandparents?

DAY 3 **Independent Practice**

Select a writing sample from a writing folder to examine the way end punctuation marks are used for different kinds of sentences. Think aloud as you decide if the paper has included different end punctuation to strengthen the writing. Allow time for editors to examine end punctuation and sentence types in their writing sample. The goal is to include a variety of sentence types to bring dimension to their writing.

 PEER EDIT Share examples of different kinds of sentences and end punctuation marks you used. Explain why you used them and how they influenced the meaning of your piece. Offer suggestions on how more variety could be added.

 SUM IT UP Remember, sentences end with different punctuation marks: declarative with periods, interrogative with question marks, and exclamatory with exclamation marks. Sentence variety makes writing more interesting to a reader.

✔ Assess the Learning

- Collect writing samples and analyze them to determine if students are independently using a variety of end punctuation marks.

- During writing conferences, have students identify examples of all three sentence types in their writing.

🔗 Link the Learning

- Have students record different end punctuation marks on each of three separate cards. Then, the teacher gives examples of declarative, interrogative, and exclamatory sentences as students quickly hold up the card displaying the correct end punctuation for the sentence.

- Create "punctuation detectives" by having writers circle periods, underline question marks, and box in exclamation points in newspapers.

- Read aloud *Yo! Yes?* by Chris Raschka. Conversations about end punctuation will spontaneously occur.

- Collect examples of great exclamatory sentences, but also caution students not to overuse exclamation marks.

- Collect examples of words that signal an interrogative sentence. *Who, what, when, where, could, should, how,* and so on are all important signal words that writers need to know.

Comma: In a Series

DAY 1 Model the Focus Point

Commas keep words from running together. They tell a reader where to pause and help separate ideas. It just wouldn't sound right if I said, *I had a chicken sandwich corn salad ice cream large milk*. Phew! I didn't get a breath because there weren't any commas! I am writing about cleaning up after dinner. Watch how I use commas. I want to tell how we *clear the table, stack the dishes* . . . .
I didn't use a comma after every word this time, did I? I need to put the comma between the groups of words. Your job is to watch how I use commas to separate words or groups of words in a series. I'll say *comma* and pause as I write a comma. Then I'll include the word *and* before the last word or groups of words in a series. Do you see how I put *and* before the last idea in my list? When I'm finished, I'll reread to proofread and edit for commas separating words or phrases in a series. I'll want to be sure I put *and* before the last idea in each list.

> **Modeled Writing Sample**
>
> ### The Nightly Routine
>
> Each night after dinner we clear the table, stack the dishes, and fill the sink with sudsy water. We washed the milk glasses, the dinner plates, and the silverware, and the pots and pans were scrubbed last. We dried them, put them away, and checked to see that everything was tidy. Washing, drying, and cleaning seemed to go on forever.

TURN AND TALK Think about how I used commas in a series. Explain how I used commas and what they tell the reader to do. Talk together about using *and*.

SUM IT UP Commas are used between items in a series. They tell you where to pause. Use the word *and*, preceded by a comma, before the last item in a list.

DAY 2 Guided Practice

On the overhead projector, place student writing that includes items in a series, or use the writing sample on page 184. If the author is one of your students, invite the author to read the selection to the class.

> June 3, 2007
>
> Dear new 2nd grader,
>
> You're going to like 2nd grade. I just KNOW it! Here are some of the cool things you didn't get to do in 1st grade. but you get to do now. You'll be able to eat your snack DURING writing, keep your water bottle on your desk and have five more minutes for lunch. Then you get to stay in the recess line until the 1st graders go in. In 2nd grade you get to do cool science experiments have pe 3 days a week instead of 2 and get to help with the k class. Be sure to bring your pencils, paper erasers and box of Kleenex by Friday. If everybody brings everything Mrs. M will give you a cool treat.
>
> Your friend,
>
> Zane P.

TURN AND TALK Discuss the meaning of the selection and offer a compliment to the writer. Now, think together about the author's use of commas. State the purpose for using commas in this writing. Point out examples of correct or incorrect usage.

If students have suggestions, ask permission from the author before implementing the changes.

SUM IT UP To a class editing chart add, "Commas separate words and phrases in a series." (Examples: *Emily's hair is long, dark, and loaded with curls. My dog has learned to sit up and beg, fetch the paper, and bring Dad his slippers.*) Remember, commas separate ideas in a series and tell the reader to pause.

DAY 3   Independent Practice

Model how to select writing to proofread and edit for commas in a series. Then have writers choose a few selections from their own folders. Give them a few minutes to proofread and edit.

 PEER EDIT Show your partner where you used commas to separate words or phrases in a series. Read your papers to each other, using the commas and pausing. Then, read your papers without pausing for commas. You will find that it is very challenging to read straight through. Why is that so? Talk about the differences. Why is it that commas are so helpful to readers? If you don't have a place where you have a series in your writing, create one in your writer's notebook.

 SUM IT UP Writers have an important job. They need to use commas to separate words and phrases in a series to be sure readers know just where to pause.

✅ Assess the Learning

- Use the tool on page 172, the Class Record-Keeping Grid: Commas, to monitor your students' use of commas in a series.

- Set up this scenario: "It is your responsibility to teach a new student to use commas to separate items in a series. Write out an explanation of what you would say. Include one example." Then, have your students meet with a younger student and share their learning about commas in a series.

Link the Learning

- Create teams of detectives who search for "Sentences With Words/Phrases in a Series." Provide collections of familiar books and sticky-note flags. Have teams flag sentences with items in a series. Then pair up teams to share their findings.

- Celebrate sensational sentences! Create a bulletin board entitled "Sentences With Noteworthy Items in a Series." Have teams search for great sentences in mentor books, then write their favorite examples on sentence strips. Once examples are posted, compare them. How many items tend to be in a series? Have they noticed the Rule of Three, often employed by authors to create a satisfying sense of balance?

- Encourage readers to continue to read with writers' eyes. Record favorite sentences with words or phrases in a series in a reader's notebook during sustained silent reading.

- Read *Alexander and the Terrible, Horrible, No Good, Very Bad Day* by Judith Viorst and compare a list of adjectives with items in a series.

Comma: After Introductory Phrase or Clause

DAY 1 **Model the Focus Point**

Note: Post a chart of "Starter Words": *when, as, after, until, before, if.*

> I see a lot of sentences that sound something like this: *I have a bike. I ride my bike after school.* When a writer begins sentences the same way, the writing isn't very interesting. Watch as I use some of these *starter words* to begin my sentences. I am going to use *when* to start my first sentence. Notice that when starter words begin a sentence, I use a comma later in that same sentence to let readers know where to pause. When I'm finished, I'll reread for meaning and then proofread for commas and starter words.

Modeled Writing Sample

When I ride my bike, I love the feel of the wind in my face. Before I start, I take a deep breath and prepare to launch. As I push off and send my pedals spinning, a huge grin spreads across my face. What a sensational feeling!

 TURN AND TALK Think together. How did my starter words affect my writing? Why is this better than short sentences that all start with *I*? What do you notice about the comma? How does it help you as a reader? Select two of the starter words and think of sentences for them. When you share your sentences, hold up your fingers to form a comma when you get to the part of the sentence that should have a comma.

 SUM IT UP Begin sentences with different words to add variety and sophistication. When using a "starter word" as the first word in a sentence, you need to help the reader by inserting a comma when it's time to pause.

DAY 2 **Guided Practice**

Place a student writing sample on the overhead projector. Use the writing sample from page 182 or a sample from your class that includes starter words or that you can edit to include starter words and commas. If the author is one of your students, invite the author to read the selection to the class.

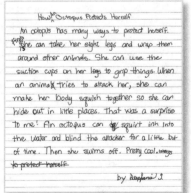

 TURN AND TALK Come up with a compliment for the author. Discuss the meaning of the selection. Think about starting sentences with different words. If starter words were used, check for commas later in the sentences. Can you insert some starter words and commas to strengthen this writing?

 SUM IT UP To a class editing chart, add "Use a comma after an introductory phrase."

Remember, writers choose different words to begin sentences. Starter words and commas later on in the same sentence make interesting sentence beginnings.

DAY 3 **Independent Practice**

Select any writing sample from a writing folder. Share your thinking as you proofread for starter words with commas in the same sentence. If none exists, look at the starter word list for editing ideas. Writers take over the process by doing the same in their own writing.

 PEER EDIT Celebrate better beginnings. Take turns reading your writing; point out starter words and commas that follow later in the sentence. Reread your writing to think together about additional places to add introductory phrases and commas.

 SUM IT UP Varying sentence beginnings by using starter words followed by a comma makes writing sound smoother and more sophisticated.

 Assess the Learning

- Confer with writers during writer's workshop to assess their understanding of using commas after an introductory clause or phrase beginning with a subordinate conjunction, i.e., a "starter word."

- During small-group instruction, assess the learners' ability to identify introductory clauses or phrases in reading selections. Have them explain the purpose of the comma that follows the phrase.

Link the Learning

- Carousel Activity: Post seven charts around the room. On each chart, write one starter word and an exemplar sentence for that word. For example, "<u>While</u> strolling through the park, . . ." Groups are assigned to charts with the goal of writing sentences using the starter and including the comma. Ring a bell and have groups rotate to a new chart with a new starter word. This will create a rich collection of sentences with strong introductory phrases or clauses followed by commas.

- Have students "collect" sentences with introductory phrases followed by a comma from some of their favorite books. Have them underline starter words.

- Students record in their writer's notebooks favorite starter word phrases from the Carousel Activity to use in their writing. Have them write favorite examples for each.

Comma: Transition Words to Show Passage of Time

DAY 1 — Model the Focus Point

Note: Post a chart of transition words. See Tools section, page 152.

There are certain words called "transition words" that help writers show the passage of time. They say, "Hey! Pay attention! Time is moving on . . . ." As I write about turtles, I am going to focus on transition words that show changes in time. Words like *once*, *while*, *soon*, *then*, or *next* all help to show that time is moving forward. These are helpful tools for a writer. When I use a transition word or phrase, I need to be sure to follow it with a comma. My first sentence starts *Once each spring*. *Once* is my transition word. Notice that I add a comma after *spring*, because that is the end of the phrase telling *when*. The comma is really important. Next, I will use *while* to show that two things are going on at once. Transition words really help me to show time. Let's reread to see how I am doing with my transition words. Good writers and editors reread all the time.

> **Modeled Writing Sample**
>
> Once each spring, a female turtle lays more than a hundred eggs. While the eggs settle, she gently spoons sand over her nest. Meanwhile, the tiny turtles mature and prepare to hatch. Soon, tiny turtles will begin to work their way toward the sea.

 TURN AND TALK Using the posted list of transition words, find transition words in my example that show passing of time. Are there any other transition words that I could have selected? If I were to keep going, which transition words would help me continue?

SUM IT UP Use transition words to alert the reader that time is moving forward. A comma usually follows a transition word or phrase.

DAY 2 — Guided Practice

Place student writing on the overhead projector. You may want to use the writing sample from page 185 or one from your class. If the author is one of your students, invite the author to read the selection to the class.

 TURN AND TALK Discuss the meaning of the selection and think of a compliment for the writer. Think together to determine if the author used transition words. Identify transition words that could be added to enhance this writing and show passage of time. Proofread and edit for commas, too.

SUM IT UP To a class editing chart, add "Use transition words to show passage of time. Follow with a comma."

Transition words alert the reader that time is passing.

> A walrus went swiming in the Ocean one day he jumt in the water and all fish swan away his tusks were sharp and long and white. they no he can eat them all in one bite.

DAY 3 | Independent Practice

Post a chart of transition words, emphasizing those that show time. Show how to select a student writing sample to proofread for use of transition words. Ask writers to select writing and to proofread for transition words followed by commas. If their writing doesn't include transition words, have them edit to include them.

 PEER EDIT Take turns identifying transition words and explaining their use in sentences. Then, read the writing with and without the transition words. Decide which represents stronger writing. Help each other add transition words to show passage of time.

 SUM IT UP Remember, writers use transition words to tell the reader that time is passing. Transition words are usually followed by commas.

✔️ Assess the Learning

- Gather writing folders and assess to see which students are integrating transition words into their writing.

- Have students identify and collect transition words in their reading selections.

⦾ Link the Learning

- Read *Wilma Unlimited* by Kathleen Krull once to enjoy this amazing biography; then, read it again to identify and pull out the transition words.

- Read *Goldilocks and the Three Bears*, a Caldecott Medal winner by James Marshall. Identify and list the transition words. You will also find great transition words in *Rotten Ralph* by Jack Gantos, *The Mitten* by Jan Brett, and *Make Way for Ducklings* (another Caldecott book) by Robert McCloskey.

- Send the students on a scavenger hunt for transition words in resources they use for independent reading, small-group instruction, and content area investigations.

- Have writers use their writer's notebook to experiment with sentences using a variety of transition words and phrases. They may want to create a rich list of transitions to keep for ready reference, as well as collect great sentences from literature that can inspire them in their use of transition words.

- Transition words support writers. Provide copies of the tool, Create Your Own Resource: Transition Words, page 152. After you have assessed it for understanding, have students complete then insert the resource into their writer's notebook.

Apostrophe: Contraction

DAY 1 **Model the Focus Point**

Let's take a look at contractions. I just used the contraction *let's*. I will write that so you can see it. Instead of writing the two words, *let us*, I used a contraction: *let's*. When we combine those two words into one word and use an apostrophe to show that one or more letters have been left out, that's called a contraction. I've decided to write an informational poem in the voices of two frogs. My frogs are hungry so I will start with *we're*. (*We + are*) I will leave out the letter *a* and insert an apostrophe. The first frog says, *I'll stretch*. That's a contraction for *I will*. I need to leave out the letter *w* in this contraction.

 TURN AND TALK Writers, talk about my poem. Now, concentrate on the contractions. Identify them, and then reread the poem and substitute the two words represented by each contraction in the poem.

 SUM IT UP Contractions combine two words into one by taking out a letter (or letters) and replacing it (them) with an apostrophe.

> **Modeled Writing Sample**
>
> Frogs Waking in Spring
>
> We're hungry
> First, I'll stretch
> I'll stretch, too.
> Let's find a meal.
> I'll go first.
> No, I'll go first!
> We'll go together.
> Sticky tongues twitch
> Mmm. Fly.
> What's next?

DAY 2 **Guided Practice**

Place a piece of student writing on the overhead projector. Use the writing sample from page 181 or a sample from your class that includes contractions or could have contractions added. If the author is one of your students, invite the author to read the selection to the class.

TURN AND TALK First, talk about a compliment you can offer the author and discuss the meaning of the selection. Now, switch your attention to the contractions. Reread the paper to consider putting in contractions. Discuss the difference in the "feel" or tone of the writing. Of course, be on the lookout for the apostrophes.

SUM IT UP To a class editing chart, add "Use an apostrophe to replace deleted letters in a contraction."

Remember, contractions are formed by combining two words and using an apostrophe to show that a letter or letters have been left out.

DAY 3   Independent Practice

Model how to select, proofread, and edit writing for contractions. Give student editors a few minutes to reread for contractions and correct use of apostrophes. Encourage them to substitute contractions if they don't have any in place.

 PEER EDIT Read each other's papers and then check for the apostrophes in contractions. Discuss your findings. Compare the contractions you each used. Give each other ideas for adding contractions.

 SUM IT UP Remember, when writers use contractions, they make two words into one by taking out a letter or letters and putting an apostrophe in its place. Contractions make our writing sound more like how we talk. They are considered less formal than writing out the two words.

✔ Assess the Learning

- Have students work in teams to think of contractions and write them on a chart. Assess understanding, and then post their charts as class resources.

- During reading, have students locate and identify contractions and the two-word version of each.

∞ Link the Learning

- Make the term *contraction* more concrete: Blow up a balloon and discuss expansion. Deflate the balloon and discuss contracting. Have students stretch out their arms and legs; then have them contract into a squatting ball position. Discuss the terms, then model contracting words from two separate words into a "contraction."

- Provide wipe-off boards. Give students contractions and have them write the two words that formed the contraction. Examples: *are not, would not, I am, we are, have not, let us, I will, will not, should not, have not.*

- Have students create a Concentration game with contractions and their two-word counterparts. Have them match the contraction to its two-word partner.

- Have students create a section in their writer's notebook for contractions, a personal resource to turn to quickly when needed.

- *It's* (*it is*) and *its* (the possessive form) are words that students often confuse. Give writers an opportunity to watch you use the two forms in sentences, showing them that there is an apostrophe only for the contraction. The possessive *its* is like *his, hers* and *theirs.* No apostrophe is needed. Have them create a page in their writer's notebook with sentences to help them remember *its* and *it's*!

Apostrophe: Possessive

DAY 1 Model the Focus Point

By adding *'s* to the end of a person's name, such as *This is Walter's bike*, writers let readers know that something belongs to only one person. When you are showing ownership for a group, the apostrophe moves to the very end of the word. *These are the boys' bikes*. I'll be writing about a toad and a frog. My first sentence is *While a frog's skin is smooth...* The skin belongs to the frog so I need to insert *'s* onto the word *frog*.

 TURN AND TALK Explain the importance of noticing possessive forms and adding an apostrophe. Together, write a few sentences that show singular possessive nouns. Save your sentences.

SUM IT UP To show that one person, place, or thing owns something, simply add *'s* to the end of the word. To show that more than one noun possesses something, just add an apostrophe.

> **Modeled Writing Sample**
>
> Comparing a Frog and a Toad
>
> While a frog's skin is smooth and moist, a toad's skin is thick, bumpy, and considerably drier. Because of short back legs, a toad's hopping ability doesn't compare to that of the strong-legged frog.

DAY 2 Guided Practice

Place student writing on the overhead projector. Use the writing sample from page 183 or a writing sample from your class. If the author is one of your students, invite the author to read the selection to the class.

TURN AND TALK Talk about a compliment for the author. What are your thoughts about the meaning of the selection? Now, decide whether and where the author successfully showed singular possession.

Receive the author's permission before implementing changes.

SUM IT UP To a class editing chart, add "Possessive: Add *'s* for singular and ' for plural."

This rule is helpful most of the time when showing possession for a noun.

> **A Cricket's Five Senses**
>
> Written by George M.
>
> Part 1: "A Cricket's Eyes"
>
> The cricket has five senses but there are distinct differences. While we have only two eyes a cricket has five. Some of the crickets eyes let him see dark and light and some of his eyes let him see in a lot of places at one time. If you think a crickets eyes are cool wait until you hear about the crickets ears.
>
> Part 2: "A Cricket's Ears"
>
> A crickets ears are not where you would expect, they are on his legs! A cricket can stretch out its legs and "hear" all kinds of noises that a persons ear couldn't pick up.

Look through a writing folder for a sample that includes singular possessive nouns. Talk aloud as you proofread for the 's. Ask the writers to look in their writing folders and select a piece of writing to proofread, and edit for singular possessive nouns.

 PEER EDIT Look over each other's paper to verify the use of 's to show ownership for a singular noun and ' for a plural. Write your names on a blank paper.

 SUM IT UP To show possession, add 's to the end of a singular noun. Add ' to the end of a plural noun.

✔️ Assess the Learning

- Have students orally demonstrate use of possessive /s/, and then assess their ability to create a piece of writing that includes possessive /s/ with an apostrophe.

- Have students flag a portion of a writing sample from their writing folder that includes singular possessive nouns or plural possessive nouns. Collect and assess for understanding. Record findings on a student checklist.

∞ Link the Learning

- Search for possessives in the hilarious *Punctuation Takes a Vacation* by Robin Pulver.

- Rewrite a modeled writing sample that includes singular possessives by turning them into plural nouns and possessives. Example: Day 1 of this cycle.

- Have students conduct a scavenger hunt for possessives by collecting the possessives in three lists: singular, plural, and possessive pronouns, such as *his*, *her*.

- Provide a sentence strip and pen to partners. Have them prepare and present a sentence that includes a possessive noun written with the apostrophe in position. Teams share their sentences with each other and then post them on a bulletin board.

- Have teams create posters with rules for possessives (singular, plural, and possessive pronoun) and post them in a visible place as tools for writers.

Comma and Connecting Words: Combine Short Sentences

DAY 1 Model the Focus Point

Note: Display today's modeled writing in a pocket chart on sentence strips.

When we write, some of our sentences sound like this, *It is a beautiful summer day. My friends and I took a long walk in the sun*. That is okay, but as writers grow, we want more sophisticated ways to express our thoughts. Watch how I use my scissors and pull these two short sentences into one sentence connected by a comma, then add the word *so*. *It is a beautiful summer day, so my friends and I took a long walk in the sun*. Notice how I used a comma after the first sentence, followed by the word *so*. A comma and connecting words help me create compound sentences that make my writing more interesting to readers. Here are two more short sentences: *We saw a bird. It flew so fast we couldn't identify its species*. Should I connect these with *and*, *but*, or *so*? Get ready to help me. Let's reread and check our compound sentences for commas and connecting words.

> **Modeled Writing Sample**
>
> **Summertime**
>
> It is a beautiful summer day, so my friends and I took a long walk in the sun. We saw a bird, but it flew so fast we couldn't identify its species.

TURN AND TALK State what needs to be done to change simple sentences into a compound sentence. What are the advantages of these longer sentences? Should every sentence be a compound?

SUM IT UP Joining two simple sentences with a comma followed by a connecting word creates compound sentences.

DAY 2 Guided Practice

Display this writing sample from page 183 and explain that it may contain compound sentences. Model how to look for complete short sentences embedded into a compound sentence by underlining the short sentences. Demonstrate how to check for a comma and connecting words so the compound sentences are correctly displayed.

 TURN AND TALK Decide which sentences should remain unchanged and which can be joined into a compound sentence. Examine the punctuation in this piece. Did the author remember to use a comma and connecting words for the compound sentences?

> **A Cricket's Five Senses**
>
> Written by George M.
>
> Part 1: "A Cricket's Eyes"
>
> The cricket has five senses but there are distinct differences. While we have only two eyes a cricket has five. Some of the crickets eyes let him see dark and light and some of his eyes let him see in a lot of places at one time. If you think a crickets eyes are cool wait until you hear about the crickets ears.
>
> Part 2: "A Cricket's Ears"
>
> A crickets ears are not where you would expect, they are on his legs! A cricket can stretch out its legs and "hear" all kinds of noises that a persons ear couldn't pick up.

SUM IT UP To a class editing chart, add "Compound sentences combine two short sentences by using a comma and connecting word."

Combining simple sentences into compound sentences makes our writing more sophisticated. Writers can join two short sentences by using a comma and a connecting word.

DAY 3 Independent Practice

From a student writing folder, select a sample with compound sentences or simple sentences that could be turned into a compound. Depending on your selection, model proofreading for compounds or editing to create compounds. Turn the responsibility over to the students and remind them to check for commas and connecting words.

 PEER EDIT Read and show each other your compound sentences. Together, try out different connecting words. Decide if they would have worked. Help each other find places where short sentences can be made into compound sentences.

 SUM IT UP Compound sentences need four ingredients, in this order: one sentence, a comma, a connecting word, and another sentence.

✔ Assess the Learning

- Ask each writer to identify and display a compound sentence from his or her own writing. Assess understanding of displayed sentences.

- Circulate during silent reading, asking individuals to identify compound sentences (and their components) in their books. Be sure to have them comment on commas and the selection of a connecting word.

Link the Learning

- In *Mechanically Inclined*, an excellent resource for middle school teachers, Jeff Anderson has created the acronym, FANBOYS, to refer to seven of the coordinating conjunctions: *for, and, nor, but, or, yet*, and *so*. We selected the four most often used, creating the acronym SOBA! Have students create personal 3" x 5" reference cards for SOBA.

- Go on a scavenger hunt through favorite picture books. Teams can collect simple sentences and rewrite them as compounds or collect compound sentences and break them down into two short sentences.

- Become sentence collectors, collecting terrific examples of compound sentences from literature. Students can use them in a special section of their writer's notebook.

SOBA
Use a comma and a connecting word to connect sentences.

| Sentence, | so
or
but
and | sentence. |

Punctuation in Dialogue

DAY 1 — Model the Focus Point

Note: With sticky notes and a pen in hand, read aloud from *Don't Let the Pigeon Drive the Bus* by Mo Willems. After each bit of dialogue, use your sticky notes to point out quotation marks, and then identify the speaker with lines such as, "whispered the pigeon."

> **Modeled Writing Sample**
>
> "Hey, can I drive the bus?" begged the Pigeon. "Please?" he whispered. "I'll be careful."

This book is great! I love the dialogue. Now that I have added my sticky notes, this book follows four rules of writing dialogue: (1) use quotation marks around the things people say out loud; (2) capitalize the first word in the quotation marks; (3) put end punctuation inside the quotation marks; and (4) identify the speaker. Let's check my first line together and see if I used all four rules. Did you notice that I tried not to use the word *said*? That word is used too much, and I want my writing to be more interesting. When I've finished, I'll reread to see if I'm satisfied with my writing; then I'll proofread to check that I used the four dialogue rules.

TURN AND TALK Think together about the four dialogue rules that writers need to follow, then check my work. We'll talk about them as a class after your partner conversations.

SUM IT UP Remember, when writing what characters say out loud, you must follow the Big Four Rules of Dialogue!

DAY 2 — Guided Practice

Note: Display a copy of the writing from page 188 on the overhead or provide copies for partners. Show students how you can use scissors to cut across the writing and make room for more text right in the middle of the piece. As the students watch, add dialogue so the author talks to the teacher.

> **Head Lice**
>
> I have this teacher She is really nice. But Some time I think She has head lice. She itches all day. And the last time for head lice check She got sent home from School. I want tell you more but it is not cool. The day She came back She had no hair and her head was bear. I think to my self how did She get the lice. I kept on thinking untell I new that I was not nice because I'm the one who gave her the lice.
>
> By: Samantha

TURN AND TALK Writers, I just added dialogue right in the middle of a piece that started without dialogue. What is the impact on the writing? Did I follow the four dialogue rules? Think together. Would you have added dialogue in a different place? Would you have used different words? How might you add dialogue to spice up some of your writing?

SUM IT UP To a class editing chart, add "Follow the four dialogue rules."

When we write the exact words that one speaker says to another, it is called dialogue.

DAY 3 **Independent Practice**

Look through student writing folders for a selection with dialogue. If you can't find one, choose writing where dialogue could be added. Demonstrate proofreading and editing for the four dialogue rules or show where you would add dialogue in a piece that has none. Then turn the job back to the writers, giving them time to identify or add dialogue in their own writing.

 PEER EDIT Start out by saying to each other, "Way to look for those four rules of dialogue!" Now, take turns reading and discussing each other's writing. Provide editing ideas if you spot a place where a dialogue rule wasn't followed.

 SUM IT UP Remember, when including dialogue, the exact words of a speaker, let the four rules of dialogue be your guide.

✔ Assess the Learning

- Collect writing samples that include dialogue. Use the Class Record-Keeping Grid: Rules of Dialogue (page 173) to record how students are progressing with the dialogue rules.

- Have students identify a favorite passage of dialogue from their reading and prepare to explain how the author applied all four rules of dialogue.

∞ Link the Learning

- Point out that in your modeled writing you challenged yourself to use words other than *said*. Brainstorm and list alternatives to *said*. Post the list in a visible place as a reference.

- Type familiar dialogue, omitting the punctuation. Have partners edit for punctuation. Debrief as a whole group.

- Make a bulletin board where readers can post sentence strips with dynamic dialogue they have found and recorded. Help them notice that there are many ways to insert dialogue into narrative selections and that there are many ways to identify the speaker.

- Do a modeled writing lesson that begins with a bit of dialogue, then shifts to personal narrative or a description, to show how a bit of dialogue can draw in a reader.

- Gather additional pigeon adventures by Mo Willems and have students use sticky notes to add rules of dialogue to the books.

- Have students conduct interviews, selecting one comment to quote word for word in their written summary of the interview. Have them present the quotation using all four rules of dialogue.

Cycles for Utilizing Space on the Page

Developing writers are often challenged by the space on a page and how to use it. They are often unsure about how far across the page to carry their text, how to use the margin, and where to create page breaks.

To assist children with use of space, we believe it is essential to highlight the way published authors have used space in picture books, enlarged texts, newsmagazines, and textbooks. We also need to think aloud about space on the page as we craft writing in front of children. Using up an entire line before moving to the next and saving room for a diagram, a caption, or a heading are all important dimensions of using writing space effectively. Hearing us talk about these print conventions and seeing us demonstrate how we make decisions about using space on the page help young writers develop their own craft.

Poetry, with its unlimited potential for arrangement on a page, invites rich conversations about space for words, margins, and visuals. Space is an essential tool we use as writers. It deserves the same careful modeling and conscious thought we apply to other dimensions of constructing text.

With mentoring from much-loved stories and a teacher who thinks aloud explicitly about the space on a page, second and third graders quickly begin to see options for space, print, and visuals as exciting opportunities for decision making and creativity.

Spacing and Form: Friendly Letter

DAY 1   Model the Focus Point

Note: There are many forms used for friendly letters. While we present one form in this sample, you may want to utilize the format shown in your state standards.

Today we'll look at the way we arrange space on a page and punctuate a friendly letter. I want you to notice the four parts of a letter (date, greeting, body, closing), their placement on the page, and the use of capitals and commas. In a friendly letter, you place the date on the left margin. Then add the greeting, *Dear Mr. Velasco*. Margins are really important, so you need to take time to think about spacing as you write your date and greeting. To begin the body of my letter, I will again return to the left with *It doesn't seem possible.* . . . To show you are finished with a friendly letter, you need to have a closing such as *Your friend* or *Sincerely*. I will choose *Sincerely*. Watch how I place the closing and my name at the left margin.

TURN AND TALK Writers, friendly letters are supposed to be. . . friendly! How did I do? Now, switch your discussion to the four parts of the letter. Can you name the parts? Read it again to notice my commas. Commas must be used in two sections of a friendly letter. What do you need to remember about a friendly letter?

SUM IT UP Writers follow specific guidelines when writing a friendly letter, such as the correct use of spacing, capitals, and commas.

Modeled Writing Sample

December 12, _____

Dear Mr. Velasco,

It doesn't seem possible that we've been in school for three months already. Your guidance and support has helped me so much during my first year at your school. I have appreciated the way you welcome my readers and writers into the office to celebrate their wonderful work and we all love it when you join us as a guest reader for read-aloud time. You are a remarkable principal!

Sincerely,

DAY 2   Guided Practice

Place a piece of student writing on the overhead projector. Use the writing sample from the appendix, page 177, or one from your class if it is written in letter form. If the author is one of your students, invite the author to read the selection to the class.

TURN AND TALK Talk about a compliment you can offer the author. What can you say about the meaning and tone of the letter? Is it friendly? Now, proofread the letter for spacing. Check to see if the four parts are located in the correct places. Look for the capitals and commas in the heading, salutation, and closing.

SUM IT UP To a class editing chart, add "Friendly letters have specific rules about spacing."

Remember to use the correct form for a friendly letter. Look at our poster of how to write a friendly letter if you forget the guidelines. Writers who are ready may add this to a personal log of editing tips.

DAY 3   Independent Practice

Have students reflect on a friendly letter they have written, looking closely at placement of parts of the letter and checking margins. Encourage them to consider capitals and commas for correct use.

 PEER EDIT Talk about the four parts needed for a friendly letter and where they belong on the paper. Then show your partner your letter. Check closely for capitals and commas.

 SUM IT UP Remember, letters require writers to follow certain guidelines. Writers have to think about spacing and margins and watch for capitals and commas.

✓ Assess the Learning

- Create a rubric or a list of expectations for an effective friendly letter; then have students assess letters to see how they did.

- Gather letters and assess spacing, inclusion of all elements, use of margin, capitals, and commas.

- Confer with writers to review their letters for conventions. Celebrate when students apply them correctly and set goals for improving conventions in future letters.

Link the Learning

- Have students make an entry in their writer's notebook with reminders about friendly letters. They may want to create a personal checklist of rules to follow and steps to consider when editing a letter. Be sure to guide them in considering voice.

- Teach students to address an envelope and have them mail letters to an authentic audience —someone in their lives or in the community, a real audience.

- Arrange for your students to write to their parents, and ask the parents to write back.

- Find another class to become pen pals with your students.

- Enjoy books with letters in them, such as *The Jolly Postman* by Janet and Allan Ahlberg or *Dear Mr. Henshaw* by Beverly Cleary.

- Visit author Jan Brett's Web site for wonderful, interactive stationery for students to use in creating their letters (www.janbrett.com/jan_brett_interactive_stationery.htm).

Spacing in Informational Texts

DAY 1   Model the Focus Point

Note: Gather an array of informational books, and as you turn pages, think aloud about the pictures and other visuals, as well as text features, such as captions, boldface words, and so on.

When authors create informational books, they plan each page so that there are visuals to help a reader understand. I have placed three sheets of paper on the wall because I am going to write at least three pages to make a book about ants. Watch as I quickly place ant facts on each page. This will help me stay focused on the purpose for each page. First, I want to think about spacing. I need to plan where to place a picture and my writing, and I need to think about a diagram, too. That would take some space but would really help my reader. I will make quick sketches to help me remember where I am putting things on each page. My first page is about ant burrows. I am thinking I should have a drawing of a burrow and that there should be labels on the drawing. I will put that at the top of the page. On my next page, I want two text boxes and two pictures. I need to think about where to put them.

Page 1	Page 2	Page 3
An ant is a tiny insect that lives in a burrow.	An ant has feelers on its head. It also has a large abdomen.	Ants have six legs.

 TURN AND TALK Writers, talk together. Writing lots of pages on the same topic is something informational writers often do. Every page isn't jammed with words; there are illustrations, diagrams, and margins that are woven thoughtfully together along with words.

 SUM IT UP Informational books combine pictures, spaces, captions, words, and so on\ to convey messages.

DAY 2   Guided Practice

Place an informational text such as Motorcross, page 189, on the overhead projector.

TURN AND TALK Writers, talk about a compliment you can offer the author. What can you say about the meaning of the selection? What do you notice about the text features and use of space? Now, think together. Could the one-page writing turn into lots of pages? What do we know about writing books with lots of pages? What might you put on page 2?

SUM IT UP To a class editing chart, add "Informational writing uses text features and visuals."

Writers, remember that informational texts use a lot of visuals, labels, boldface text, and diagrams to work with the words and help a reader understand the message.

DAY 3 Independent Practice

Select a piece of modeled writing that consists only of words and show students how you can cut it into sections, placing each section on a new page. This leaves room for visuals and other text features that are important in informational writing. Encourage your students to discuss the cutting-up process and how it enhances the presentation of ideas in informational texts.

 PEER EDIT Show your partner an informational writing selection and talk about how you can cut it up to add text features and turn it into a multiple-page book. Think together about how you could use space and visuals.

 SUM IT UP Informational writers plan their texts carefully and use space to insert diagrams, illustrations, captions, headings, and the other features that work with the writing to convey facts and information in a clear and engaging way.

✓ Assess the Learning

Send students on a scavenger hunt through informational texts, identifying and listing text features they find. Then, have them review their own work in their writer's notebook and writing folder to see how many of those same text features they have incorporated in their own writing.

🔗 Link the Learning

- Keep a list of text features that you see most often in your students' writing. Gather small groups of writers and model using additional text features to broaden their range.

- Create multiple-page books with carefully designed features and publish them to display in the school library or office.

- Write and edit alphabet books such as the Ocean Alphabet, the Desert Alphabet, or the Alphabet of Amphibians as another way to extend your students' thinking about multiple-page informational books.

- Help writers to explore use of space in procedural texts (e.g., directions), looking closely at space, formats for numbering, diagrams, lists of materials, and so on.

Cycles for Moving Forward With Spelling

It has been well proven that spelling is developmental, that it grows hand–in–hand with print knowledge in reading and in writing. In addition to print knowledge, children need to have *strategies* for navigating the challenges of crafting meaningful print with spelling that can be read by others. When writers approach spelling tasks strategically, they have a sense of when to rely upon themselves and their own knowledge of letters and sounds, and when to go to the word wall or to a personal resource such as a portable word wall. (See Spelling Strategies Self-Assessment, page 165.) Because strategic spellers know how to navigate their work in word building, they pay attention to the way words look and notice patterns in words. Strategic spellers have a distinct sense of *spelling consciousness* that guides them in their writing.

Spelling Strategies Self-Assessment

Writer_____ Date _____

Mark the strategies you use: (Put a star next to the ones you use the most)

- ❑ Stretch words out slowly and listen to sounds
- ❑ Draw a line under words I am not sure of during drafting or write sp
- ❑ Clap out the syllables and check each syllable for a vowel
- ❑ Try to visualize what the word looks like
- ❑ Use another piece of paper or the margin to spell the word several ways
- ❑ Use words I know to spell other words
- ❑ Use a portable word wall
- ❑ Use the class word wall
- ❑ Refer to the tricky words and homophone lists
- ❑ Use a dictionary
- ❑ Use a thesaurus
- ❑ If I know I can find the word quickly, I might _____
- ❑ If I think it will take me some time to find the correct spelling, I wait until editing, then I might _____
- ❑ During editing, ask a friend to edit with me
- ❑ During editing, add words to my portable word wall that I think I will use again

When I come to a word I am not sure of during drafting, I usually _____

or _____. During editing, I would follow up on the word

by checking _____ or _____

If you were to give advice to a younger student about spelling, what would you tell

that writer? _____

_____

Spelling Consciousness

DAY 1 — **Model the Focus Point**

Note: Prepare this writing sample in advance.

Today, our focus is on "spelling consciousness." This means that writers pay attention to spelling even during first drafts. If writers aren't certain about a spelling, they underline the word or write a little *sp* above the word. Writers should never think that spelling isn't important. It is. What is important is that writers try not to stop writing to check a dictionary or wait for help while they are in the middle of writing. The best writers use words that sing with meaning, even if the spelling is tricky! Thinking of the best words, rather than being stuck with words you can spell correctly, will help you be sure your writing is worthy of reading. Let's look at my writing and notice the words where I used my spelling consciousness to identify tricky words. I don't let spelling get in the way of choosing the best words for my writing!

 TURN AND TALK Talk to each other about why writers should not stop to look up words in a dictionary when they are writing their first draft. Think about marking words to return to them later. Do you prefer to underline the word or write a little *sp*?

SUM IT UP When writing a first draft, if you're uncertain about the spelling of a word, quickly draw a line or write an *sp* above the word. This reminds you to choose terrific words and find the spelling later.

Modeled Writing Sample

Varoom

When I was a youngster, Saturday was clean-the-house day. My favorite chore was vaccuming. I loved hearing the VAROOM of the vaccum as it started up and the tick-tick-tick-tick-ticking of dirt being sucked up into the belly of the machine. Sometimes my cat would saunter in, flop down, and wait to be vacuumed. He thought being vacuumed was absolutely delicious.

DAY 2 — **Guided Practice**

Place a piece of student writing on the overhead projector. Use the writing sample from page 176 or select a writing sample from your class. If the author is one of your students, invite the author to read the selection to the class.

TURN AND TALK Talk about the meaning of the selection and offer a compliment to the author. Did the writer pay close attention to spelling? How do you know? Decide together: Which words deserve closer attention and should be marked with an *sp*?

My fat Tail Lepord casy Geko has a fat tail. I hold hime every day. Some times he climes on my bed. his name is Jake. hise favorit thing to eat is meal worms. He lvis in a ten golen fish tanck. He has a lot of room. hise favorit things to do are eat slepe a stee still.

SUM IT UP To a class editing chart, add "Draw a line or write *sp* when you aren't sure of spelling."

If you're not sure about a spelling, quickly underline the word or write *sp* above it. Keep writing! After writing, look up spellings.

DAY 3 | Independent Practice

After you've modeled the process of selecting a rough-draft writing selection from a writing folder and then proofreading to make certain you've identified uncertain spellings, turn the process over to the students. Their goal is to reread a rough-draft writing, looking for evidence of spelling consciousness and marking *sp* above or underlining any other words that may be misspelled.

 PEER EDIT Share your thinking about spelling consciousness, what it is and why it is important. Point out the words that have *sp* above them. Make changes if you know the correct spelling. Help each other think of ways to find correct spellings for words during editing.

 SUM IT UP If you are writing a word and you aren't sure of the spelling, quickly underline the word or write *sp*. After writing, return to verify or correct spelling.

✔ Assess the Learning

- Observe writers during their first-draft writing. Using a class record-keeping grid, check off writers whose papers show evidence of spelling consciousness.

- Interview editors individually and have them explain spelling consciousness.

Link the Learning

- Have editors record the correct spelling of tricky words in alphabetized multi-page personal references. The problem area of a word should be highlighted, underlined, bolded, or broken into helpful chunks to aid spelling (e.g., Feb *ru* ary).

- If homophones cause a spelling quandary, write homophones within context sentences. Provide students with Spelling Reference: Tricky Words and Homophones, page 149.

- Teach students to think of the richest, best choices for words and never be tempted to stick to words just because they know how to spell them.

- Model spelling consciousness while writing in front of students. Show them how you underline or record *sp* above possible misspellings but keep going and maintain your thought. After writing, return to the underlined words and use a resource to check your spellings.

Syllable Rules for Spelling

DAY 1 — Model the Focus Point

Today, I'll share two rules about syllables that will help us spell. First, when we say *animal*, we hear three parts or three syllables: *an*, *i*, and *mal*. Breaking words apart and hearing their syllables helps us spell them. Second, every syllable has at least one vowel, so *animal*, with three syllables, has to have at least three vowels, one in each syllable. (Spell a̲n- i̲- ma̲l.) Your job is to watch me use these syllable rules to help me spell. When I've finished, I'll reread my writing for meaning and then check that I used the syllable rules. I've decided to write a poem about fish.

Modeled Writing Sample

Darting flashes

Quivering and alert

Fins slicing

Jaws snapping

Hungry no longer

For the moment

 TURN AND TALK First, discuss my poem. Which lines were your favorites? Now, think and talk about the spelling strategies I used. What did you see and hear me doing?

 SUM IT UP Writers break words apart into syllables to help spell the parts. Then they check that each syllable always has at least one vowel.

DAY 2 — Guided Practice

Place a transparency of student writing on the overhead projector. You may use the writing sample from page 184 or use one from your class. If the author is one of your students, invite the author to read the selection to the class.

> Dear Mrs. Hoyt,
> Thank you for everything. I loved the way you did things also I liked the web of understanding it was cool. I had fun with everything. I hope you have a good trip Home to oregon.
> Love,
> Kala
>
> Read books.

 TURN AND TALK Writers, talk about the meaning of the selection and think of a compliment for the author. Now, switch your focus to spelling. First, tell each other the two syllable rules that help writers spell. Does the writer understand these rules? Give multiple examples from the writing to support your answer.

SUM IT UP To a class editing chart, add "Break words into syllables. Each syllable has at least one vowel."

Remember, break words into syllables and always have at least one vowel in each syllable.

DAY 3 | Independent Practice

Select a paper from a student writing folder and then reread it to ensure that the writer included a vowel in every syllable. Ask the writers to proofread and edit their selected writing for vowels in every syllable.

 PEER EDIT Partners, take turns proofreading each other's papers to verify that each syllable has at least one vowel. Then decide if you are automatically (1) putting at least one vowel in each syllable and (2) breaking words into syllables to help your spelling. It's now up to you to use these syllable rules each time you write.

SUM IT UP Check that each syllable has at least one vowel. Break words apart into their syllables to help spell the parts.

✔ Assess the Learning

- Observe editors at work. Use a class record-keeping grid to record which students break words into syllables and check that each syllable has at least one vowel.

- Interview students who still need to internalize these key strategies. Find out exactly what they know.

Link the Learning

- Based on your observations, gather students into brief guided writing experiences where you guide them in the use of the syllable rules.

- Provide small-group instruction with texts that students can read independently. Have students collect words with one, two, and more syllables, and then check the words for vowels.

- Have your students teach a younger student how to use the syllable and vowel rule.

- Use a pocket chart to display multisyllable words and engage students in helping you cut the words into syllables before checking for a vowel in each syllable.

- Have teams make posters of terrific multisyllable words and post them around the room to encourage your students to develop a sparkling vocabulary that is not limited by spelling concerns.

Try Unknown Words Several Ways: Margin Spelling

DAY 1 Model the Focus Point

As I write today, I'll focus on a spelling strategy called "margin spelling." If a word doesn't look quite right, I'll quickly rewrite it a couple of different ways in the margin. If I recognize that one of my attempts is correct, then I'll cross out the incorrect spelling in my writing and write the correct spelling above it. If the spellings all look wrong, I will just draw a line through them and jot *sp* above the word so I remember to go back and check it later. When I've completed my writing, I'll go back to edit for spellings of words that were tricky.

TURN AND TALK Talk about the specific things you saw and heard me doing to help me with tricky spellings. Write them down in a bulleted list that you will later share with another team.

SUM IT UP Use margin spelling during writing to quickly try different spellings of tricky words.

> **Modeled Writing Sample**
>
> A Turquoise Sky
>
> While flying home from a
> business trip, I gazed out
> into an exceptionally beauti-   tourquise
> ful day. The ~~terquoise~~ sky   terquoise
> tourquise was dotted with
> puffy clouds that looked   cumullus
> like cotton balls. ~~terquoize~~   cumulus
> ~~Cumulous~~, nimbus or what-
> ever the cloud was called,
> ~~cumullus~~ it was beautiful to
> me. cumulus

DAY 2 Guided Practice

Place a piece of student writing on the overhead projector. Use the writing sample from page 185 or a writing sample from your class. If the author is one of your students, invite the author to read the selection to the class.

 TURN AND TALK Consider the writing's meaning. Think of a compliment for the author. Now, look for evidence of margin spelling. If you were this writer's spelling buddy, what specific feedback would you offer? How would margin spelling have helped?

SUM IT UP To the class editing chart, add "Use margin spelling for tricky words."

Writers need quick ways to help them spell during writing.
Trying to spell a tricky word a few ways in the margin is one strategy worth trying.

> A walrus went swiming
> in the Ocean one day
> he jumt in the water
> and all fish swan away
> his tusks were sharp
> and long and white.
> they no he can eat
> them all in
> One bite.

DAY 3 | **Independent Practice**

Model how to skim, by running your fingers over a text, to check for potential spelling errors. Then model writing a few margin spellings for a tricky word. Turn the responsibility over to the students to do the same with their writing.

 PEER EDIT With your partner, I'd like you to compare your margin spellings. What do you notice about the tricky words? Does it help to look at different examples? Share specific rules or observations you made.

 SUM IT UP Margin spelling is a strategy worth using. When you are stuck on a word, quickly try a few different spellings to see which one looks best to you.

✅ Assess the Learning

- Student editors write their names on a sticky note and record one of the words they margin-spelled. Collect notes on a chart paper. Analyze the error patterns that you observe.

- Using a class record-keeping grid, check off writers whose papers show spelling attempts in the margins.

🔗 Link the Learning

- Utilize the Teacher Resource: High-Frequency Writing Words tool, page 147. They are the words that appear most often in writing and are also those most commonly misspelled. Help students gain control over these and watch their confidence soar!

- Model sticky-note spellings with spelling patterns you want to emphasize for students. Example: During modeled writing, use large sticky notes to practice changing the *y* to *i* and adding *es* for plurals (e.g., *puppy* to *puppies*, *party* to *parties*). When students see you apply spelling rules in a strategic and thoughtful way, they will be more likely to try it as well.

- Challenge writers to utilize terrific words in their writing, and then use margin spellings to give it a go! Celebrate "courageous spellers" who reach high and use words that sparkle.

- Provide writers with "Give It a Try" sheets you make to use during writer's workshop and encourage them to try spelling words in various ways during editing before turning to a dictionary. They can then see how close they came to the dictionary spelling.

Portable Word Walls

DAY 1 · Model the Focus Point

Note: Use the Spelling Reference: Portable Word Wall tool, page 148.

Take a look at this portable word wall. I know I will use this resource a lot, so I have slipped it into a sheet protector to keep the pages readily at hand. I use my portable word wall during drafting if I am sure I can find a word fast! If I am not so sure, I wait until editing to check the word. I don't want to slow down my thinking by stopping too often to check spelling. I am going to write about the neighbor's cat becoming a mother. I am thinking about the word *became*. I will look in the *b* section really fast to see if it is here. It isn't here, so I will get right back to my story and keep writing. To finish my sentence, I want to use the word *mother*. That's a word we use a lot. I bet it is on my portable word wall! Let's check and see.

TURN AND TALK Writers, talk about the things you saw and heard me doing to help spell. Then I would like you to discuss one thing that I never did. (I never stopped writing to wait for help.)

SUM IT UP Use a portable word wall as a quick reference during writing, but most of the time, use it after you have finished.

> **Modeled Writing Sample**
>
> Wish Me Luck
>
> The cat next door just bee came a mother. She had three babies with shiny, coal black fur and two with short, spiky brown hair. As soon as my mom and dad get home, I'm going to ask them if I can hav one. Wish me luck!

DAY 2 · Guided Practice

Place student writing on the overhead projector. Choose the writing sample from page 179 or one from your class. If the author is one of your students, invite the author to read the selection to the class. Provide each student with a portable word wall from the Tools section, page 148.

TURN AND TALK Talk about a compliment you can offer the author. What can you say about the meaning of the selection? Use a portable word wall to proofread and edit for spelling. Do you think the writer used a portable word wall to proofread and edit the writing? Why or why not?

SUM IT UP To a class editing chart, add "Use a portable word wall during and after drafting."

Writers usually use a portable word wall to check spelling *after* writing, but they sometimes use it during writing, too.

> **Bus Rides**
> by J.D.
>
> I ride on a skool bus just like every body els. It seems to take for ever. I hav to get up by 6:30 to cach the bus by 7. Win its rainy and cold, the frist bus step can be xtreemly slippery. Since my little sister and me are the frist on the bus we get to sit on the bak seat. Its like a xtra long bench. She sits by one windo and I sit by the other. We look out the windo and wach cars zip by. Then we do the same thing on the way home. Its sort ov boring but its better then waking.
>
> I ride on a **skool** bus just like every body <u>els</u>. It seems to take for ever. **I hav** to get up by 6:30 to *cach* the bus by 7. **Win** its rainy and cold, the **frist** bus step can be <u>xtreemly</u> slippery. Since my little sister and me are the frist on the bus we get to sit on the back seat. Its like a <u>xtra</u> long bench. She sits by one <u>windo</u> and I sit by the other. We look out waching the cars zip by. Then we do the same thing on the way home. Its sort ov boring but its better then *waking*.
>
> Note:
> - **Bolded words** are on the personal word wall, Appendix 2.2. (**school, when, first, of**)
> - <u>Underlined words</u> would probably remain "sounding out" words unless the piece was to be published. Then the teacher would act as editor to correct remaining spelling errors.
> - *Italicized words* could be added to JD's Personal Word Wall (*Catch, walk*)

DAY 3 Independent Practice

Select writing that includes words that second and third graders often misspell. Briefly show students how to proofread and edit using a portable word wall, then have them select writing to proofread and edit using their portable word walls.

 PEER EDIT Show your partner places where you checked and/or corrected spelling. Together, recheck each other's papers for spelling errors using your portable word walls.

 SUM IT UP A portable word wall can help you *quickly* spell some words during writing, but it's best saved for after writing.

 Assess the Learning

- As you observe editors, use a class record-keeping grid to document those who are making progress with portable word walls, using them primarily after writing and occasionally during writing.

- As you confer with writers, ask them to show you how they use their portable word wall and tell when it is most effectively used.

Link the Learning

- Use the Teacher Resource: High-Frequency Writing Words tool, page 147, to determine appropriate words for portable word wall references. Most writers will have the same list, while a few may need a longer or shorter list. Portable word walls should change over the course of the year as students gain proficiency.

- Challenge writers to spell words from their portable word wall correctly in daily writing.

- Provide parents with copies of portable word walls to support writing at home.

- Have your students take dictation from kindergarten students, using their portable word walls to assist them in spelling for their young friends.

Pulling It All Together

For learning to be long lasting, children need opportunities to explore their understandings in more than one context. The Power Burst Lessons and Pulling It All Together Cycles are designed to provide interactive experiences in which children can review conventions and mechanics they have recently explored. These experiences are not designed to teach new content, but rather to review and support the transfer of knowledge to other contexts.

There are two parts to this section:

Power Burst Lessons: These are learning experiences that fit nicely into small windows of time. When you have 10 minutes, slip in one of these interactive experiences and review recently addressed conventions and mechanics.

Pulling It All Together Cycles: These are fully developed cycles that are linked to the yearlong planner and designed to tie together multiple points of learning. These cycles are designed to provide intensive review of three weeks of learning within the context of an authentic writing purpose that has a real audience.

Power Burst Lesson: Secret Sentences

To create secret sentences, write each word and punctuation mark of a sentence on individual sheets of paper, one word or punctuation mark per piece. Have teams of students (each student holding one piece of paper) move themselves around to arrange their words and punctuation into a sentence that begins with a capital letter, ends with a punctuation mark, and expresses an idea that makes sense.

With second and third graders, you might begin with sentences from quality literature selections shared during read-aloud time. Familiar lines energize conversations and give students confidence in navigating sentences.

As students gain experience with secret sentences, you can branch out to less familiar sentences that challenge their sense of grammar and meaning more fully. Choose secret sentences that provide a review of grammatical structures, recently learned mechanics, spelling rules, and conventions. Complex sentences linked with connecting words and commas also work well as secret sentences.

For additional diversity, consider deriving sentences from sources like these:

- students' writing
- science and social studies content
- experiences in class
- rules for positive behavior in class
- playground rules
- current events
- mathematics concepts

As their confidence grows, students can start to work in pairs to create secret sentences for their peers to reconstruct.

Power Burst Lesson: Scavenger Hunt

Select a writing convention or issue of mechanics that you've focused on in a recent cycle and explain to students that you are going to search a picture book to find the convention or issue in context. Think aloud as you review the selected book and celebrate each time you find an example. As you move through the selection, tally the number of times you find exclamation points, question marks, sentence openers followed by a comma, and so on.

Once students are familiar with the scavenger hunt idea, have individuals, partners, or reading teams survey big books, whole-class reading selections, small-group guided reading selections, weekly magazines, newspapers, and so on, keeping a tally of their findings. As they continue to gain more skill in conducting scavenger hunts for differing items, encourage students to work with partners to conduct a scavenger hunt through their own writing folders.

Power Burst Lesson: Tricky Word Dramatics

Create Tricky Word teams and give each team a set of cards labeled with tricky words or homophones, such as *hair* and *hare* or *buy*, *by*, and *bye*. Your students' task is to create a way to dramatize their tricky words so the audience can determine which words they are dramatizing.

- During the performance, the cards labeled with tricky words or homophones should be displayed to assist the audience.

- After the performance, have partners come up with sentences using the tricky words or homophones.

For the Writer's Notebook

Students create a special tabbed section in their notebooks for tricky words and homophones. They can keep a running list of tricky words with corresponding context sentences that help them identify the correct meaning. They also might want to add a sketch for quick identification during drafting or editing.

Some Tricky Word examples to consider		
our	hour	
by	buy	bye
for	four	
hair	hare	
know	no	
they're	their	there
to	two	too
your	you're	

Power Burst Lesson: Combining Sentences

Research suggests that students become more proficient writers when they learn to combine short sentences. Beginning writers often construct sentences sounding something like this:

Lions are strong. They have big paws. The lion is the king of the jungle.

In Combining Sentences, the objective is for students to get involved in the action. Place short sentences written on sentence strips in a pocket chart; then show how you can cut up the sentences and combine the words in new ways to create richer, more interesting statements. Be sure to place punctuation marks and connecting words (*and, but, although*) on individual sentence strips so their presence is very obvious. Your creations might sound something like this:

The <u>big paws</u> *and* <u>strong</u> body of the waiting lion made it clear that he was <u>king of the jungle</u>.

With his <u>big paws</u> in a relaxed pose, the <u>strong</u> body of the lion made it clear that he was <u>king of the jungle</u>.

Lions have <u>big paws</u> *and* <u>strong</u> bodies that have earned them a reputation as <u>king of the jungle</u>.

Lions have <u>big paws,</u> *but* it is their <u>strong</u> body that has earned them the title "<u>king of the jungle</u>."

Guided Practice

Provide pairs of students with two short sentences on sentence strips. Have them cut the sentences apart with the goal of combining the sentences, adding more words, and creating one sentence that is longer and more interesting. Point out that adding commas and connecting words will help them as they combine sentences. Have them post their new sentences in a pocket chart.

Alternates

- Provide students with compound sentences written on sentence strips. Have them cut the sentences apart and create two shorter sentences.

- Have students search through favorite books to find compound sentences (sentences with two independent clauses linked by connecting words). They write their sentences out on a sentence strip, then rewrite them as two shorter sentences.

Power Burst Lesson: Check It!

Explain to students that the best editing checklists are often those they create themselves. When they create their own checklists, they can incorporate strategies they are currently working on and think about the purpose and audience for the pieces they are editing.

Work together with students to draft an editing checklist for an authentic writing purpose, such as a letter to their parents, an invitation to an event at school, or a report that will be read by others.

Post the editing checklist on a chart and have students test it. Revise the checklist based on students' findings from their writing samples. Type the checklist and provide copies for your writers to use as they prepare their work for an audience.

Power Burst Lesson: Headlines

Newspaper headlines are often incomplete sentences, meant to convey a message quickly. Let students know that, in this exercise, their job is to turn headlines into interesting sentences that convey clear messages.

Display a headline from a newspaper or magazine, asking students to write sentences of their own based on the headlines. Students can share their sentences with classmates after they focus on both the message and the mechanics. Use this opportunity to discuss the parts of a complete sentence.

You can extend the lesson by challenging students to expand the headlines based on lessons that have recently been introduced. Depending on the headlines chosen, students' needs, and your instructional goals, you might ask students to include elements such as the following:

- adjectives that compare
- adjectives that make the writing sparkle
- plural nouns
- proper nouns
- possessive nouns

Two key questions for identifying a complete sentence:
Who or what did something?
What did they do?

Power Burst Lesson: Sort It Out

This lesson is designed to help students sort words, sentences, and/or sentence parts into categories. Share this exercise after one of the cycles, focusing the sorting on that particular skill or strategy you have just covered. Using familiar sentences from literature, have students cut up the sentences, begin to sort words or phrases into appropriate categories, and then discuss the sorting with the whole group.

Students can sort for all kinds of words, sentences, and fragments, including the following.

- Present-tense verbs and past-tense verbs: Students can sort and then work together to change verbs from present tense to past tense.

- Singular nouns and plural nouns: To add an extra challenge, you might instruct students to change singular nouns into plural, or plural nouns into singular. Attention would then need to be placed on subject-verb agreement.

- Common nouns and proper nouns.

- Titles with correct word capitalization and titles with incorrect word capitalization: Provide strips labeled with titles on them, some correct and others incorrect. Have students correctly capitalize words in the titles with mistakes.

- Nouns and pronouns: Replace names with corresponding pronouns (*Mr. Henry/he; Sally/she; the students/they*).

- Action verbs and linking verbs: Create a T-chart with "Action Verbs" and "Linking Verbs" as headings. Then students can write verbs on sticky notes to place in the proper place on the chart. You can write the verbs on sticky notes yourself and ask students to place them correctly.

- Complete sentences and sentence fragments: Write sentences and fragments on sentence strips for students to sort. Provide an extra challenge by having students rewrite fragments into complete sentences.

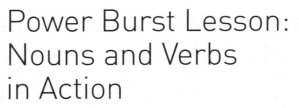

Power Burst Lesson: Nouns and Verbs in Action

Remind students that nouns stand for a person, place, or thing, while action verbs represent motions and actions.

Explain that they need to be on their feet and ready to move when you call out directions. They will hear you say either "Touch a noun" or "Dramatize a verb!" With two students to help demonstrate, model how to appropriately touch a person, place, or thing for "Touch a noun." Then, use charades to pantomime actions when you call "Dramatize a verb!" Be sure to give the students time to tell a partner the nouns and the verbs they are dramatizing.

Power Burst Lesson: Interest Inventory

Interest inventories give students authentic purposes for considering what interests them. When students interview peers, adults in the school, parents, and others, they capture authentic data that provides them with a purpose for utilizing what they know about capitalization, punctuation, spacing, and so on. The interest inventory requires students to apply so much of what they have learned about conventions and mechanics that it makes a perfect Pulling It All Together opportunity.

We suggest that they begin by completing the inventory about themselves and then branch out to interview a classroom partner. After that, they can take their inventories on the road, interviewing school-based personnel, parents, relatives, students from other classes, and so on. The inventories can be placed in a class book and accompanied by a digital photo of each interviewee.

See the Tools section, page 158, for a template of this inventory or work with your students to create your own!

Interest Inventory

Name _____ Date _____

Date of birth _____ Number of siblings _____

Siblings' names: _____

	Your favorite:	Your least favorite:
• pet:		
• color:		
• food:		
• beverage:		
• restaurant:		
• subject:		
• book title:		
• author:		
• sport:		
• sports team:		
• theme park:		
• actor/athlete:		
• other:		

Where have you lived?

• city and state _____

Hobbies/interests: _____

List important qualities in a friend: _____

Write whatever you would like to add: _____

Pulling It All Together Cycle #1: Thank You Letter

Spelling Consciousness • Use an Editing Checklist • Portable Word Walls

DAY 1 | Model Writing for an Audience

This week we had something exciting happen in our class. We got a visit from Mr. _____, who told us all about his job. I want to write a letter to thank him for visiting. He was a special guest, so I want this letter to be the best that it can be. I am going to be careful to use what I know about spelling consciousness and then use my editing checklist and portable word wall to help myself. In this first sentence, I want to use the word *you*. Sometimes that word is tricky. It doesn't look like it sounds. But it's on my portable word wall, so I can quickly check the spelling and move on. I don't want to stop while I'm writing to check spellings of other words, because I want the ideas to flow. Mr. Johnson is a herpetologist. That's a tough word, and I'm not sure I spelled it correctly. So I'll put a little mark—*sp*—above it and check it later. I think that word was on his business card, so I can check it there when I proofread. Finally, I'll look at my editing checklist. I'll reread one time for capital letters at the beginning of sentences. Then I'll reread to check to be sure I have the right punctuation mark at the end of each sentence. I'm glad I checked! I forgot the question mark at the end of our sentence in quotes.

> **Modeled Writing Sample**
>
> Dear Mr. ____,
>
> Thank you for visiting our class this week. When you left, we were disappointed that we forgot to ask our most important question: "What's your favorite part of being a herpetologist?" Please come back soon!
>
> Sincerely,
>
> Mr. Simonsen

TURN AND TALK Writers, talk about my "thank you note." I had three goals in mind. I wanted to use spelling consciousness, my portable word wall, and an editing checklist. How did I do? Think together about how I used each of those tools.

CREATE AN AUTHENTIC PURPOSE Have students write a thank you note to someone. Remind them to use their portable word walls, mark words with spellings they are unsure of, and reread for each proofreading and editing point. To keep the writing experience authentic, be sure that students have an opportunity to deliver their notes or actually mail them.

ASSESS THE LEARNING As students write, identify those who may need additional support in using strategies for spelling words correctly and those who need more instruction in focused editing and proofreading.

SUM IT UP Writers, we created thank you notes while using portable word walls, editing checklists, and showing we were thinking about spelling. You know how to think about spelling while you write, and you know strategies for checking your work to make sure we have capital letters and punctuation. When we send our letters, we'll know that we have done our best!

DAY 2 | Guided Practice

MODEL: HOW TO APPLY THE LEARNING TO DAILY WRITING Select an example of modeled writing. Read it aloud and invite students to point out any words with spellings that they are unsure of. Mark those words with *sp* and then follow up by checking them later. Then model using an editing checklist and rereading for each editing point. Through your demonstration, show that the editing process makes the writing easier to read.

 TURN AND TALK Writers, think together about what I just did.

 CREATE AN AUTHENTIC PURPOSE Have students select pieces from their writing folders to reread with a checklist. Have them read through the first time to identify words with spellings about which they are unsure. Then have students edit together with partners, referring to portable word walls as needed.

 ASSESS THE LEARNING Meet with small groups and observe them closely. Note which students are demonstrating spelling consciousness as they write. Determine which of your students can use an editing checklist effectively and which are utilizing portable word walls during and after writing.

 SUM IT UP We are working hard to make our writing the best it can be. We think about spelling while we write, but we make sure to put our ideas on paper and then check the spelling later. We use a special set of strategies like a tool belt to improve our writing on each read-through. Now, turn and tell your partner how using a checklist, a portable word wall, and spelling consciousness makes your writing even better.

DAY 3 | Support and Extend the Learning

Select experiences that will best support your learners:

- Encourage students to work with you to create the editing checklists that best serve their goals and instructional needs. Focus on checklists with several related points rather than many unrelated points to keep the checklists manageable for students.

- If students prefer not to mark their writing with *sp* as they write, encourage them to use sticky notes to mark tricky words or draw a line under words that need attention.

- Work with students to create portable word walls for the content areas, such as often-used words in math, science, social studies, and so on.

- Encourage students to write thank you notes often. They could, for example, write notes to thank each other for help with an assignment. They might write notes to school staff members thanking them for something special they did. Remind students that letters make an impression and that when they thank someone, they want their work to be the best it can be. Suggest they write their notes on "From the Desk of _____" on page 157.

Pulling It All Together Cycle #2: Readers Theater Script

Syllable Rules for Spelling • Comma: After Introductory Phrase or Clause • End Punctuation: Period, Question Mark, and Exclamation Point

DAY 1 | **Model Writing for an Audience**

Note: Have a copy of *Click, Clack, Moo: Cows That Type* by Doreen Cronin available.

Let's create an interview with the characters of this story and then write a Readers Theater script. I'll start with a question to the farmer. *When you went to the barn, what did you notice? When you went to the barn* is an introductory phrase, so I need to place a comma before I write *what did you notice?* We have been working on introductory phrases, haven't we? I also need to put a question mark to show this is a question. I'll write two more questions and answers. I am having a little trouble remembering how to spell *letter*. I am going to clap the syllables in *letter*. I hear two syllables. Each syllable needs a vowel. How did I do? Now, let's read this dramatically. . . .

 TURN AND TALK Writers, talk about my Readers Theater script. I tried to use three important things: syllable rules, an introductory phrase and a comma, and end punctuation. How did I do?

 CREATE AN AUTHENTIC PURPOSE Students can work in pairs to write a set of questions and answers about another book that they can turn into a Readers Theater experience. Remind students to carefully check end punctuation, insert an introductory phrase and comma, and be sure they have a vowel for each syllable. Have partners rehearse their script in preparation for an actual presentation to an audience.

✓ **ASSESS THE LEARNING** Confer with individual students and check their writing samples for end punctuation, commas after introductory phrases, and a vowel in each syllable.

☺ **SUM IT UP** Writers, we put together a script that will be so much fun to read! We thought about end punctuation and introductory phrases with a comma, and we used what we know about syllables to be good spellers.

Modeled Writing Sample

Interviewer: When you went to the barn, what did you notice?

Farmer Brown: I noticed that the cows weren't giving milk.

Interviewer: What surprised you the most?

Farmer Brown: I couldn't believe that cows could type a letter!

Interviewer: After the cows got their blankets, what else happened?

Farmer Brown: Those darn ducks wanted a diving board.

DAY 2 | Guided Practice

MODEL: HOW TO APPLY THE LEARNING TO DAILY WRITING Select an example of modeled writing. Demonstrate looking carefully at end punctuation to be sure that you have used the correct punctuation marks. Then go back and check the spellings of a few of the words. Show students how you clap the syllables and then check to be sure that each syllable has a vowel. Finally, check to see if there is a sentence with an introductory phrase and a comma.

 TURN AND TALK Writers, how did I check the spelling of some of the words I didn't know? How did this strategy help me to become a better speller? What strategies did you see me use to choose the correct end punctuation? Which strategies do you use to figure out what punctuation to use?

 CREATE AN AUTHENTIC PURPOSE Have students select pieces from their writing folders to reread. Encourage them to find a place or two where they can add excitement by including an exclamation point. On a focused rereading, invite students to hone in on spelling, using the strategy of clapping out syllables and checking each syllable for a vowel. Finally, challenge them to find an introductory clause and a comma to add one to their writings.

✔️ **ASSESS THE LEARNING** As students reread and edit, have side-by-side conferences to assess their use of end punctuation marks, commas after introductory phrases, and the presence of a vowel in each syllable.

🙂 **SUM IT UP** A punctuation mark is a signal to a reader, and you are learning to give your readers great signals. Are they reading a question, a statement, or something really exciting? You are helping them by carefully choosing end punctuation. When you use commas to set off introductory phrases, you show that you understand how good sentences are created. Checking your spelling by using syllables is just one more thing you are doing to make your writing clearer for your readers.

DAY 3 | Support and Extend the Learning

Select experiences that will best support your learners:

- Provide appropriate opportunities for students to clap out syllables. They can also cut words into syllables, pull the words apart, and put them back together.

- Create a cloze activity by duplicating sentences on an overhead transparency, leaving off the end punctuation. What punctuation belongs at the end of the sentence? How do students know? Engage them in conversations about the possibilities.

- Give students index cards, with one form of punctuation on each of the cards. Read a sentence aloud and have students hold up the correct end punctuation card.

- Provide sentence stems that are introductory phrases, such as *When I was walking down the street, After lunch, As the sun set on the horizon,* and so on. Have partners think of ways to complete the stems and then write their sentences on sentence strips to display.

- Ask students to read the same group of words with different end punctuation and discuss the change in meaning. Example: *Those tacos are hot. Those tacos are hot? Those tacos are hot!* Students may enjoy creating similar sentences.

Pulling It All Together Cycle #3: Classroom Signs

Reread During Writing and Editing • Complete Sentences vs. Fragments • Commas: In a Series

DAY 1 Model Writing for an Audience

I've been thinking about our new science center. It's been a lot of fun learning about liquids and solids. But I want to create a sign to make sure that we have the right materials and are all safe when we work there. I want to say, *You need a pencil, paper, and your science book.* That sentence lists three items in a row so I need to be sure to put a comma between *pencil, paper,* and *science book.* Now, I will check to see if it is a complete sentence: Does it tell who? Does it tell what to do? Notice how I keep rereading to check my work. That is important. Next, I could say, *Clean up spills. Put used paper towels.* Oops! That was a fragment. I need to tell where to put the towels, so I will write, *Put used paper towels <u>in the trash</u>.* Good thing I am rereading and editing as I write! I'll write a third rule and when I am finished, I will read very carefully again to check my work. Finally, we are ready to place the sign in the science center to help us remember how to stay safe there.

> **Modeled Writing Sample**
>
> **Stay Safe in Our Science Center!**
>
> 1. You need a pencil, paper, and your science notebook.
>
> 2. Clean up spills. Put used paper towels in the trash.
>
> 3. Don't taste anything in the science center.

TURN AND TALK Talk with your partner about my writing. How did it help to proofread and edit while I was writing? How did I handle commas in a series and checking for fragments? Think together.

CREATE AN AUTHENTIC PURPOSE Gather ideas for classroom safety signs or other signs that would be helpful for the classroom. Have teams create signs that will actually be posted in the room. As they work, remind them: *Check for fragments. Use commas for items in a series. Reread during and after writing.* Confirm that teams reread their work as editors before writing their work on "final" posterboards for display.

ASSESS THE LEARNING

- Observe students closely as they write; create a list of students who need additional support in writing complete sentences.

- Provide authentic situations in which your students use commas in a series, then assess for understanding.

SUM IT UP Writers, let's take a look at these signs. They will remind us to be safer and work together in our classroom, and this will help us create a great place to learn! Let's think together about what we know how to do. We proofread and edit while we write, not just when we are done, so we are always thinking about what we're putting on the page. We know how to place commas in a series of items, and we write great sentences that aren't missing any parts.

DAY 2 | Guided Practice

MODEL: HOW TO APPLY THE LEARNING TO DAILY WRITING Gather a selection of modeled writings that you have done for students. Select one to edit. Reread it and think aloud about the sentences. Read the sentences to make sure that they are complete, with no fragments. Look for items in a series, and share your thinking as you place or point out the commas between the items. Finally, show students how you proofread and edit to make sure that the message is easy for readers to understand.

 TURN AND TALK Writers, what did you see me do when I was checking for fragments? Did you notice how I asked the two important questions: *Who or what did something? What did they do?* What is the function of commas when we write items in a series? How would it help you to proofread and edit while you write instead of waiting until you are finished?

 CREATE AN AUTHENTIC PURPOSE Have students look through their writing folders to find a piece that needs a second look. Encourage students to ask the two important questions that we ask when verifying if we have a complete sentence or not. Remind them to use commas for items in a series. Finally, allow time for students to share their work with partners to discuss improvements they made through editing.

 ASSESS THE LEARNING Review writing samples to determine who can write complete sentences and use commas with items in a series.

SUM IT UP We are becoming better writers all the time. Our sentences make sense, and we are thinking about the commas writers use to separate items in a series. We are also remembering to proofread and edit while we write, not just after we are finished writing. When we pay careful attention, our writing gets better and better!

DAY 3 | Support and Extend the Learning

Select experiences that will best support your learners:

- Provide sentence fragments on strips of paper. Challenge students to identify "what's missing" (a subject or a verb) and rewrite the fragments as complete sentences.

- Work with students to create small "reminder checklists" that they can use as they proofread and edit. You might make them the size of bookmarks so that you can laminate them and place them on students' desks.

- Work with the idea of items in a series by playing a memory game. Place common class objects on a tray and show all the students. Then hide the tray from view. Students can write about what they saw, e.g., *I saw a pencil, an eraser, a stapler, a calculator, and a bottle of glue.* Students' sentences should include commas.

- Safety signs may be needed in other areas of the building, such as on stairs, in the lunch line, on the playground, and so on. With permission from school administrators, allow students to create other safety signs for the building. These signs need to be edited for 100 percent accuracy since they are being posted.

Pulling It All Together Cycle #4: Classroom News Report

Sentence Parts: Subject and Verb • Pronoun Order: Person's Name and Then *I*, Not *Me*
• Pronouns: Clarify Meaning

DAY 1   Model Writing for an Audience

Each week, I send home a class newsletter. For this edition, I want to write about the nature walk and how we took a closer look at our environment! First, I need to start with the *who* of the story—*I* led the class on a walk. But I know I can't start by saying *I and the students*. I need to say, *The students and I*. . . . I need to be polite and list others first. Next I might tell what we did. *We noticed plants, animals, and insects.* Let's think about that sentence. Does it have a subject? The subject is *we*. It tells who the sentence is about. Does the sentence have a verb? The verb is *noticed*. It tells what we did. This sentence has a subject and a verb, so it's a complete sentence. The word *we* needs attention as well. *We noticed.* . . . Is it clear who *we* refers to? Will the reader know I mean *the students and I*? Writers have to be sure a reader understands who is being talked about.

> **Modeled Writing Sample**
>
> Taking a Closer Look
>
> By Mrs. Wilson
>
> The students and I took a walk through our school habitat to fine-tune our powers of observation. We noticed plants, animals, and insects. With a focus on looking and really listening, we realized that there were bees buzzing near colorful flowers.

TURN AND TALK Talk with your partner. Pick a sentence and identify the simple subject and the simple verb. How does finding the subject and verb help you write a better sentence? Talk about the pronouns in the writing. Could you tell what each pronoun was referring to?

CREATE AN AUTHENTIC PURPOSE Let students know that they will work with partners to write an article about a classroom event to add to the class newsletter for parents. Encourage writers to verify that each sentence has a subject and a verb. When they include pronouns, they need to stop and ask, *Is this clear? Will the reader know who the pronoun is naming?* Remind students who write about themselves and others that it is polite to list the names of other people first.

ASSESS THE LEARNING

- As partners write their articles, check their work to identify those who might need extra assistance with identifying and including both subjects and verbs in their sentences.

- Gather writing samples to identify those who may need assistance with pronouns and antecedents.

SUM IT UP Writers, your articles will make an amazing newsletter to send to your parents. You remembered to write sentences that have subjects and verbs. Remember— if you have a pronoun in your writing, stop and ask yourself, *Can my readers figure out who or what this pronoun refers to?*

DAY 2 | Guided Practice

MODEL: HOW TO TRANSFER LEARNING TO ANOTHER CONTEXT Model how to select a piece of writing from your writing folder and reread to check for clear pronoun referents, sentences that include both simple subjects and simple verbs, and correct order of words in the subject. As you identify these elements in the writing, think aloud and share your ideas about adjustments that you need to make.

 TURN AND TALK Writers, what did you see me do as I checked my writing? Talk about why it is helpful to look for subjects and verbs in sentences. What are you doing to help yourself remember the two key questions for confirming a sentence is complete? How can pronouns help our writing? How can pronouns make writing confusing?

 CREATE AN AUTHENTIC PURPOSE Students look through their writing folders to find a piece of writing that might need a second look at the sentences. Have partners work together to identify the simple subjects and simple verbs in the sentences. Remind them that if they cannot find both a simple subject and a simple verb, they should rewrite the sentence. Students can also search for pronouns and make sure the pronouns clearly refer to particular nouns.

 ASSESS THE LEARNING As partners work together rereading their writing, assess which students need extra support identifying simple subjects and verbs and correctly using pronouns.

SUM IT UP Newsletters give important information, so you have done a valuable job and created a wonderful resource for your parents! You have used strategies to write stronger sentences, and you are using pronouns in a way that makes sense. We keep adding tools to our tool belts of writing strategies. Great job!

DAY 3 | Support and Extend the Learning

Select experiences that will best support your learners:

- Encourage students to report on events in their town, school, and global community.

- Students enjoy reading and writing jokes. Have students write jokes with a noun in the joke and a pronoun in the punchline so that the jokes show clear antecedents. Examples: What game do elephants like to play? They like to play squash! Why did the farmer bury his money in the soil? He wanted rich fields!

- Cut sentences apart into simple subjects and simple verbs. Students can reassemble them in pocket charts and identify the subjects and the verbs.

- Students can play a game to match nouns with pronouns. Create cards with both nouns and pronouns and have students match them. For example, *the teachers* matches *they*, *Mr. Murphy* matches *he*, *the lemur* matches *it*, and so on.

- Encourage students to go on a pronoun hunt using a piece of text you are reading. As an added challenge, write the pronouns on one side of a T-chart. On the other side, students can write the noun or nouns that are referred to by each pronoun.

Pulling It All Together Cycle #5: Announcement Letter

Capitalize for Emphasis • Spacing and Form: Friendly Letter • Comma: Transition Words to Show Passage of Time

DAY 1   Model Writing for an Audience

I was thinking about the game we're making for the Fun Fair. I want to write an announcement about it. I am going to write a short letter the principal can share with the school. After I write *Dear Students*, I need to remember the comma. In the first sentence, I'll tell what our game is. Now, I want to tell what we will be doing, so I will begin with *First*. *First* is a transition word, so I need to insert a comma after it. My next sentence is *Then, you will.* . . . I used another transition word and a comma. I also want to add some excitement to the writing, so I'll put *SPLASH* in all capital letters to add emphasis. This sounds great! Let's reread the announcement to make sure it shows that our game is fun and exciting.

> **Modeled Writing Sample**
>
> Dear Students,
>
> We are excited to announce our fishing booth at the Fun Fair on Saturday! First, you'll get your very own fishing pole to cast into the prize pond. Then you will thrill to the SPLASH as you cast, and wait in excitement to see what an amazing prize you will get.
>
> Sincerely,
>
> Ms. Brent's class

TURN AND TALK Talk about the modeled writing with your partner. What makes this announcement a friendly letter? Where did I put commas in my writing? Think together about why I used commas and capital letters. What did you think about the word *SPLASH*? How did you read that aloud?

CREATE AN AUTHENTIC PURPOSE Students can choose a classroom event to describe for others in an announcement letter. They could write about a fun fair, a science fair, a special guest, a games day, an at-home reading challenge, and so on. Encourage students to use the form of a friendly letter and to think of a place where they might want to convey excitement by writing in all capital letters.

ASSESS THE LEARNING

• Use your class record–keeping sheet to identify students who may need assistance with the form of a friendly letter.

• During writing conferences assess understanding of the use of all-capital-letter words to generate excitement or the use of commas after transition words.

SUM IT UP Our announcement letters provide exciting information. In our letters we were able to capitalize for emphasis and use exclamation marks, transition words, and commas. We know how to use the form of a friendly letter, too. I think we are ready to share these announcement letters with an audience.

DAY 2 Guided Practice

MODEL: HOW TO TRANSFER LEARNING TO ANOTHER CONTEXT Choose a friendly letter from modeled writing that you have done with the class. Model checking for correct form of a friendly letter. Then, think aloud: *What could I do to make this writing even more exciting? Here it says, "We heard a loud noise." What if I wrote, "CRASH! We were startled by a loud noise."? That is more exciting to read.* Rethink and revise your writing using mechanics and conventions to lift the sample.

 TURN AND TALK Writers, what are some things that all friendly letters have in common? Now, talk about the word written in all capital letters. How does that word change the meaning and the sound of the writing?

 CREATE AN AUTHENTIC PURPOSE Ask partners to list the qualities of friendly letters and to find each of these elements in their own friendly letters. If any elements are missing, they should add them. Encourage writers to look for a place where they could add excitement by adding a word in all capital letters.

 ASSESS THE LEARNING

- As partners reread their writing together, identify students who may need assistance with the form of a friendly letter.

- Review your students' writer's notebooks to check that they are using commas after transition words and interjections within sentences.

SUM IT UP Writers, we have learned to write a friendly letter—a very useful skill! And we know that capitalizing a single word adds emphasis. We are doing a great job of putting commas in the right places and using transition words, too.

DAY 3 Support and Extend the Learning

Select experiences that will best support your learners:

- *SHHH! BANG! OUCH!* Write interjections with exclamation marks on index cards and distribute them to students. At appropriate times as you read a story, point to a student with a card and invite the student to read the word, with drama. Students will enjoy creating their own stories in which they can "interject!" Examples: *Too Much Noise* by Ann McGovern, *Kitten's First Full Moon* by Kevin Henkes, *Casey at the Bat* by Ernest Thayer, *Officer Buckle and Gloria* by Peggy Rathmann, and *Jumanji* by Chris Van Allsburg.

- Invite students to write friendly letters to other students in class or to pen pals in other classrooms. Encourage letter recipients to reply to those friendly letters.

- Have students write recipes. Brainstorm transition words that suggest order, such as *first, next, then.* As students draft, remind them to put commas after transition words.

- Distribute a passage from a favorite picture book to teams. Students can work together to consider adding a word in all caps for emphasis. Allow time for students to share their work with the class.

Pulling It All Together Cycle #6: Book Review

Punctuation in Dialogue • Capitalize Titles and Headings • Adjectives to Lift Descriptions

DAY 1 | **Model Writing for an Audience**

A book review is a great way to find out what others think about a book. I am going to write a review of *Jumanji* since we all enjoyed it so much. As I write, I need to remember to capitalize the title, even if the title is in the middle of the sentence. I'll start: *Chris Van Allsburg's book* Jumanji *keeps a reader's attention from start to finish.* I thought about writing that this story is exciting, but the word *exciting* is not a very sparkling adjective—it's way overused. I think I'll use *exhilarating*. That sounds like an adventure! Hmmmm . . . what else will make my review interesting? Oh, I know. I asked my friend Jose what he thought of the book, so I can quote him in the review. I need to put his exact words in quotation marks. After I'm finished, I'll check my writing. I want to be sure that I have included interesting adjectives, capitalized the title of the book, and put Jose's exact words in quotation marks. I'll put the review in our classroom library next to the book.

> **Modeled Writing Sample**
>
> Chris Van Allsburg's book *Jumanji* keeps a reader's attention from start to finish. What makes this book so exhilarating? In this fast-paced adventure, students discover a game that becomes dangerous! My friend Jose said, "I would be terrified to find a python in my living room." I agree! *Jumanji* is more than a book. It's an adventure!

TURN AND TALK Writers, talk about my writing. What adjectives showed you my strong feelings about this book? What did I do in my writing to show someone's exact words? How can you tell that *Jumanji* is the title of a book? Would my review make you want to read this book if you haven't already read it? Why or why not?

CREATE AN AUTHENTIC PURPOSE Ask students to work with partners to write book reviews. They should first interview each other and write down their partner's quotes about the book. Then, as they draft, they can include the quotation as well as replace tired adjectives with adjectives that are awake and lively. Writers need to consider adjectives that add color and zip to the writing.

ASSESS THE LEARNING Gather the book reviews and assess them for quotation marks, capitalization of the title, and interesting adjectives. Record the data you gather for future writing conferences.

SUM IT UP Today you created great reviews and you used many strategies that you have learned. You remembered that the title of a book needs to begin with a capital letter. You used adjectives that made your reviews exact and drew the reader in. And when you quoted others, you gave them credit for their words by putting the words in quotation marks. I can't wait for you to share your reviews with others!

DAY 2 | Guided Practice

MODEL: HOW TO TRANSFER LEARNING TO ANOTHER CONTEXT Choose a piece of modeled writing and hone in on adjectives by marking each adjective with a sticky note or noting places where you could add an adjective. Pause and ask, "Is there a better adjective to put here?" Demonstrate revising and adding adjectives for clarity and interest.

 TURN AND TALK Writers, what did you see me do with adjectives? How did using the sticky notes as a tool help me identify possible words to change? How might a quotation improve this writing? What do you think about adding a quotation to my writing?

 CREATE AN AUTHENTIC PURPOSE Have students look for pieces to revise in their own writing folders. They might identify adjectives with sticky notes on a first reading, and then reread to see which adjectives should be added or replaced to create vivid and specific descriptions. Encourage students to also look for places where they should enclose a speaker's exact words in quotation marks.

☑ **ASSESS THE LEARNING**

- As students reread their pieces as editors, watch for those who may need extra support with adjectives, quotation marks, and the capitalization of titles.

- Meet with small groups to interview students and check for understanding.

 SUM IT UP Editors, we are becoming "masters of mechanics!" It takes a lot of skill to choose the best adjective in writing, and we are learning how to include adjectives that give readers a clear picture or idea. We know how to put someone's words in quotation marks and to use a capital letter when writing titles.

DAY 3 | Support and Extend the Learning

Select experiences that will best support your learners:

- Place a piece of writing on chart paper or on the overhead. Encourage students to work in teams to find "tired" adjectives and replace them with lively ones.

- Create "adjective helper" posters. At the top of each, write an overused adjective, like *nice* or *good*. Students can suggest alternatives, write them on sticky notes, and place them on the posters. The posters can be an ongoing project.

- Students can keep a list of their favorite books, adding to these logs throughout the year and making sure to capitalize book titles correctly.

- Show examples of headings in trade books or in content area texts. Supply pieces of text in which the headings have been omitted. Have students read the text and supply appropriate headings, capitalizing important words in the headings. Students can also add headings to writing in their folders or their writer's notebooks.

- Ask students to imagine a meeting between two characters from well-known tales, such as Cinderella and one of the Three Little Pigs. They can write dialogue between these characters. Remind them to use the correct punctuation as they think about what these characters would actually say to each other.

Pulling It All Together Cycle #7:
Math Writing: Poster

Adjectives: Comparative and Superlative Forms • Singular Subject-Verb Agreement
• Plural Subject-Verb Agreement

DAY 1 Model Writing for an Audience

In math, we've been comparing the sizes and weights of objects, so I'm going to make a poster that compares some objects in the classroom. I'll start with *small, smaller, smallest*. A book is small. I'll write that in the first square. Now, I need to find something small<u>er</u> than a book. I can use pencils! I'll write a sentence like the first one: *The pencils is small<u>er</u> than the book*. But this sentence doesn't sound right! The word *pencils* is plural, so I need to use *are*. *The pencils <u>are</u> small<u>er</u> than the book*. Now for the third box, pennies would work. I remember that when I compare two or more things, I add *-est* to the adjective. I think I will write, *A penny are the smallest*. I think I goofed again. If I use *are*, I need a plural subject. *Pennies <u>are</u> the small<u>est</u>*. I will add more examples and proofread before I display my poster for an audience.

> **Modeled Writing Sample**
>
> The book is small.
>
> The pencils are small<u>er</u> than the book.
>
> Pennies are the small<u>est</u>.
>
> *You may want to add sketches for each example.

TURN AND TALK Writers, what ending did I add to the adjective *small* to compare two things? What about when I was comparing more than two things? Which of the subjects is singular? Which is plural? How did I have to change the verb when the subject was plural? Practice building sentences like mine. Find something small and then another item that is smaller. Think together about your sentences.

CREATE AN AUTHENTIC PURPOSE Have students work with partners or in small groups. Assign each group a word that describes size or weight, such as *tall, heavy, big, short, light,* and so on. Explain that they will be building posters like yours but will add objects of their own selection. Remind them of the rule to add *-er* or *-est* to comparative adjectives that are single syllable. Remind them also to identify their subjects as singular or plural and to choose the correct verb. Note: Multisyllable adjectives are usually compared by using *more* and *most* or *less* or *least*. A few modifiers have irregular comparisons.

ASSESS THE LEARNING
- As students work with their partners or groups, note which students are having difficulty remembering to use *-er* and *-est*.
- During individual conferences, identify students who are still confusing singular and plural verb forms.
- Be especially mindful of your ELL students, who may likely need additional instruction.

 SUM IT UP When we compare the sizes or weights of objects, we need to add special endings to our adjectives. When we have more than one object, it's important to use a verb that matches the plural form of the noun.

DAY 2   Guided Practice

MODEL: HOW TO TRANSFER LEARNING TO ANOTHER CONTEXT Choose a piece of modeled writing from previous writings you have done. Cut it apart and place the sentences into a pocket chart. Using sentence strips and scissors, model how to change a subject from singular to plural or plural to singular, and then adjust the verb to its correct form.

 TURN AND TALK Writers, what does it mean when you talk about a singular noun? A plural noun? What did you see me doing to the rest of the sentence as I changed the subject from a singular noun to a plural one? How did the verb change?

 CREATE AN AUTHENTIC PURPOSE Have students look for pieces to revise in their own writing folders. Ask them to underline the subjects of their sentences and determine if they are singular or plural. Then carefully recheck the verbs to make sure that they have used the correct forms.

 ASSESS THE LEARNING

- As students reread their writing, check to see that they understand subject-verb agreement.
- Meet in small groups with students and have them describe items in the classroom using comparative adjectives. Identify those who need continued oral and written practice with comparative forms.

 SUM IT UP We are growing as writers, proofreaders, and editors every day! Using the correct form of the verb helps our writing sound polished. We are matching nouns and verbs so that they work well together in well-crafted sentences. And when we compare, we are using the correct forms. Let's celebrate all that we can do!

DAY 3   Support and Extend the Learning

Select experiences that will best support your learners:

- Give students objects or pictures of objects and have them write sentences that compare these objects. Remind them to use the superlative form of the adjective when comparing three or more items and the comparative form when comparing only two.

- Display adjectives and their comparative and superlative forms (e.g., *small, smaller, smallest; tall, taller, tallest; lovely, more/less lovely, most/least lovely*). Have students utilize these forms in a piece of writing.

  ### Appreciating the Pond

  The sparkling waters of a pond camouflage rich and diverse life forms. <u>Small</u> otters play among the wet edges of the bank while <u>smaller</u> tree frogs hide patiently among the leaves, hoping for a tasty insect to come near. From the <u>smallest</u> minnow to the largest predator, the pond is a rich and varied habitat.

- Label index cards with singular and plural nouns and singular and plural forms of verbs, one word per card. Have students match nouns and verbs that make sense together; then craft sentences that include those simple noun and verb constructions.

Pulling It All Together Cycle #8: Summarizing Learning

Verbs: Present and Past Tense • Apostrophe: Possessive • Single vs. Double Subjects

DAY 1 Model Writing for an Audience

I am going to write a summary of what we are observing in science. I am thinking I could write, *Yesterday, we watch the crayfish to see how it changed*. But that doesn't sound right. Yesterday is in the past, so I need to change the verb—it should be *watched* instead of *watch*. Remember how the crayfish started to shed its exoskeleton yesterday? I could say, *Our class, we stared in amazement as our crayfish wriggled out of its exoskeleton*. Oops! The subjects are the same thing (*our class* and *we*)! I need to name the single subject once, so I will use *our class*. In my last sentence, I talked about the crayfish's exoskeleton. Did you notice I remembered the *'s* to show the skeleton belongs to the crayfish? Read with me as I proofread and check this again.

> **Modeled Writing Sample**
>
> Yesterday, we watched the crayfish to see how it changed. Our class stared in amazement as our crayfish wriggled out of its exoskeleton. What will we notice about the crayfish's new exoskeleton as we observe today?

TURN AND TALK Writers, what are some things you noticed while I wrote this summary? How did my verbs help me show past tense? How did I show that the exoskeleton belonged to the crayfish? How many times do you mention the same subject in a sentence? Why?

CREATE AN AUTHENTIC PURPOSE Have students work with partners or in small groups to draft summaries about a math lesson, a science lesson, an independent reading, a weather report, a special activity, and so on. Have them share their summaries with each other so there is an authentic audience for their work, or post the summaries in the science, math, and reading areas of the room.

ASSESS THE LEARNING

- As students craft their summaries, circulate and note which students are having difficulty using the correct verb tense, adding *'s* to show possession, and naming a single subject only once in a sentence.

- Collect finished summaries and assess them for understanding of the target conventions.

SUM IT UP Writers, you have created summaries that help us reflect on and remember what we have learned. You included correct verb tenses, added *'s* for possessives, and watched to be sure you didn't have any double subjects such as *The snail, he. . . !*

DAY 2 Guided Practice

MODEL: HOW TO TRANSFER LEARNING TO ANOTHER CONTEXT Read a mentor book such as *The Relatives Came* by Cynthia Rylant and, after a few pages, have the students decide if the verbs are past tense or present tense. Begin collecting great examples of past-tense verbs as you continue through the story, pausing to jot them on chart paper.

 TURN AND TALK Writers, what did you notice about the verbs that Cynthia Rylant chose? Think together. If you were to write a summary of this book, what verbs would you be sure to include? Would they be past or present tense? Which possessives with 's would you include in your summary?

 CREATE AN AUTHENTIC PURPOSE Students can look in their own writing folders to find pieces to revise. Encourage them to carefully consider if the piece is written in the present or past tense and to be sure they use the same tense throughout the piece. Invite writers to use possessive nouns, when appropriate, making sure to include apostrophes.

 ASSESS THE LEARNING

- As students reread their writing, confer with them to be sure they understand that past-tense verbs are used to describe something that already happened and present-tense verbs describe events happening right now.

- Survey writing folders and notebooks to see if students used apostrophes with possessive nouns.

😊 **SUM IT UP** We are learning how to create great summaries! We know that it's important to use the correct verb that indicates past or present tense. We realize that we only need to mention the same subject once in a sentence. We can show ownership by adding an 's at the end of a singular noun.

DAY 3 Support and Extend the Learning

Select experiences that will best support your learners:

- Have students write possessive phrases to describe things in the room, such as *Anthony's pencil*, *Cara's desk*, *Lupe's coat*, and *the class's calendar*. They can write these phrases on sticky notes to use as labels in the room.

- Read a familiar book aloud, randomly inserting double subjects. Students can raise their hands or give a signal when they hear double subjects. Volunteers can restate the sentences with single subjects.

- Have students work in groups to list words that signal the use of the past tense, such as *yesterday*, *last week*, *this past Monday*, *long ago*, and so on. They can add to this list of signal words, culling additional words from various classroom texts.

- Have students survey favorite books for possessives with 's and past- or present-tense verbs.

Pulling It All Together Cycle #9: Invitation Letter

Comma and Connecting Words: Combine Short Sentences • Spacing and Form: Friendly Letter • Single vs. Double Subjects

DAY 1 Model Writing for an Audience

Our reading buddies have been a big help to us this year. I was thinking it might be fun to celebrate our special friendship by inviting our buddies for a treat in our classroom. I want to write a friendly letter to invite them for a cookie break! I remember that I start a friendly letter with the word *Dear*. Then I'll move on to the beginning. *It is great to have you as our reading buddies. We learn a lot from you.* These ideas could be connected in one sentence. I need to replace the period at the end of the first sentence with a comma and add a connecting word. I'll use the connecting word *and* before I put these two sentences together. Now I need to give the details about our cookie break. *Our class, we would like you to join us for cookies.* As I'm writing this, I notice that my sentence has two subjects, and they are the same. I only need to name the subject once, so I'll change this. A few more details about the time and place of the cookie break, and the invitation is all set! Because this is a letter, let's be sure to write a closing. Now we can deliver our invitations.

> **Modeled Writing Sample**
>
> Dear Mr. Littlejohn and class,
>
> It is great to have you as our reading buddies, and we learn a lot from you. Our class would like you to join us for cookies! Please come to our room Tuesday afternoon after lunch. We are excited to show you how thankful we are for all your help this year.
>
> Sincerely,
>
> Mr. Bennett's class

TURN AND TALK Writers, what about my writing shows you that it is a friendly letter? How did I take two ideas and connect them in one sentence? I accidentally wrote a double subject. I named the subject twice. What did I do to make it a single subject?

CREATE AN AUTHENTIC PURPOSE Have students plan a quick classroom event that calls for an invitation. Then in small groups have them create invitations. Remind students to use the correct form of a friendly letter. As they write, have them ask themselves, "Are there small sentences that could be combined?" Remind them to put commas and connecting words between the combined sentences.

ASSESS THE LEARNING
- Use a Class Record-Keeping Grid (page 170) as you circulate to assess students' understanding of using commas and connecting words in compound sentences.
- Gather evidence from their folders to assess their ability to write a friendly letter in correct form and to avoid the use of double subjects.

SUM IT UP Your invitation letters are so well written, I know the people who receive them will be excited to attend! Using the correct form of the friendly letter shows that you care about the person you have written to. You included some compound sentences, and that makes your writing flow and sound more natural. Great job on taking out or not including double subjects! You know you don't need to say the same thing twice.

DAY 2 Guided Practice

MODEL: HOW TO TRANSFER LEARNING TO ANOTHER CONTEXT Look through your previous modeled writing pieces to find a friendly letter. As you model the editing process, check the form of the letter for a greeting, closing, and correct comma use. Model choosing two shorter sentences and combining them into a compound sentence as you take away the period and add a comma and a connecting word. Think aloud as you eliminate any double subjects in your writing.

 TURN AND TALK What did you see me do? Did you notice that I checked for each part of the friendly letter and added parts that were missing? What did I do to combine sentences? What do you look for when you decide which sentences to connect in your writing?

 CREATE AN AUTHENTIC PURPOSE Students can look through their own writing folders to find pieces of writing to reread. If possible, they should find a friendly letter and check for the correct components of friendly letters. Encourage them to find at least one place in their writing where they can connect two smaller sentences to form a compound sentence.

 ASSESS THE LEARNING

- Gather letter-writing samples from students to review the parts of the letter and check for understanding of the proper format.
- Assess students' ability to combine two short sentences to make a natural-sounding compound sentence.

SUM IT UP When we write a letter or an invitation, we want to make a great impression on the person who receives it. When you pay special attention to the form of the letter, the crafting of the sentences, and the subjects of your sentences, you make a great impression. Way to go!

DAY 3 Support and Extend the Learning

Select experiences that will best support your learners:

- Provide short sentences for students to combine. You can write the sentences on sentence strips and give them to partners or groups, who can then put the sentences together and then rewrite them with commas and connecting words.
- Write sentences that have double subjects and compound subjects (e.g., *My mom, she* and *My mom and my dad*). Put the sentences on cards so that students can sort them into piles of correct and incorrect. Students can then rewrite those sentences with incorrect double subjects.
- Have students write an advice letter to a character they have read about. Remind them to include the parts of a friendly letter, including the greeting, closing, and a signature. Students will enjoy sharing their advice letters with classmates.

Pulling It All Together Cycle #10:
Personal Narrative

Punctuation in Dialogue • Apostrophe: Possessive • Use Copyediting Symbols

DAY 1 Model Writing for an Audience

A personal narrative is a reflection from one small episode in your life. I am going to write about my first time riding a horse. I will include some dialogue, so I need to put quotation marks around the words someone said. [Think aloud as you write an episode such as the one included at right.] Now that I am finished, I want to use my editor's eye and go back and take another look. I use copyediting symbols to show changes that I need to make or that I made. I left out a word in the first sentence. I use this little mark, a caret, to show where I need to add *right* between *foot* and *there* so it says, *Just put your foot <u>right</u> there*. . . . Mr. Layne's name should start with a capital, so I will simply add a capital letter. If I were proofreading another writer's paper, I'd underline the first letter in his name three times. That would remind the writer to capitalize when he or she finished editing.

> **Modeled Writing Sample**
>
> "Just put your foot there in the horse's stirrup," soothed Mr. layne.
>
> I hoisted one foot over and glanced down at the horse. She wasn't running quite yet! I was excited but a little nervous. I hadn't ridden before, and the horse I had been assigned looked like she wanted to run! I took a deep breath and climbed aboard.

Caret: ∧

See Copy Editor's Symbols, page 156

 TURN AND TALK Writers, what did you notice while I was writing the dialogue? How can you tell that those are the words of someone else, not me? Now take a look at the word *horse's* in the first sentence. What belongs to the horse? How can you tell? Now talk about my editing. Why are copyediting symbols helpful to writers? Which symbol did I use in my own writing? Which additional symbol would I have used if I was proofreading another writer's paper?

CREATE AN AUTHENTIC PURPOSE Ask students to select a small moment and write a narrative that makes the moment come alive for a reader. Be sure they understand that they will need to include a bit of dialogue from their memory. Compile the narratives into a class book and have students take turns bringing the books home to share with their families. Remind them that dialogue will make their stories more lively and interesting. In preparing final drafts, students should use copyediting symbols as they edit and when they proofread another writer's paper.

ASSESS THE LEARNING Assess drafts and final copies of the narratives to see that your students are using the appropriate punctuation for dialogue, 's for singular possessive, and copyediting symbols in a final version or when proofreading another writer's paper.

 SUM IT UP Sharing personal stories can be fun, especially when we do our best writing to bring those stories to life! You have done a fantastic job of including dialogue—that really helps readers picture the scene. And you made your writing shine by not only using copyediting symbols, but also by following up on the items you found to change.

DAY 2   Guided Practice

MODEL: HOW TO TRANSFER LEARNING TO ANOTHER CONTEXT Find a piece of modeled writing to share with the class. Look for a place where an exact quotation would enliven the writing and make it seem more real. Show how to use the correct punctuation as you insert the dialogue into an existing piece of writing. Follow the same procedure with a possessive noun. Demonstrate explicitly how you use copyediting symbols as signals to plan a second draft of your writing.

 TURN AND TALK How do you take what someone says and write it to show the speaker's exact words? How do you think using dialogue makes your writing more exciting? How do you include copyediting symbols in your drafts or while proofreading other writer's papers?

 CREATE AN AUTHENTIC PURPOSE Have students work with partners to select pieces in their writing folders that would benefit from an infusion of dialogue. Encourage them to work together as they correctly insert and punctuate dialogue. Have them trade papers and use copyediting symbols as they proofread.

 ASSESS THE LEARNING

- Gather the revised writing selections and assess the new dialogue.
- Review writer's notebooks and folders to see that your students are using *'s* to form possessives.

 SUM IT UP You must be so proud of your work! You have used dialogue to make your stories more exciting and realistic. You also paid attention to using possessive nouns. And what about those copyediting symbols? I think they are fun and useful, too. But, even more important, they show writers what to do to make writing even stronger!

DAY 3   Support and Extend the Learning

Select experiences that will best support your learners:

- Have students reread favorite books to find examples of compelling dialogue. Have them copy their selected examples onto sentence strips with appropriate punctuation and display the strips on a bulletin board celebrating dialogue.

- Show students a literature selection with an indirect quotation (e.g., *My mom told me that I should I clean my room*). Write it on a sentence strip, and then rewrite the indirect quote as a direct quote so the students can compare the language and punctuation.

- Provide sentences in which some of the words ending in *'s* are plural and some of the words ending in *'s* are possessives. Students then find and correctly punctuate the sentences.

- Provide plenty of practice in using the copyediting symbols to mark up familiar texts that you have rewritten on chart paper or on a transparency with inserted errors. Engage students in discussing the changes, then present the original text for comparison.

Pulling It All Together Cycle #11: Creating a Brief Report

Adjectives: Comparative and Superlative Forms • Adjectives to Lift Descriptions • Capitalize for Emphasis

DAY 1 • Model Writing for an Audience

I am going to write a brief report about my favorite rock. I just love its name—it's called dog tooth calcite! And when you look at its picture, you can tell how it got its name. It looks just like a dog's tooth! I am going to compare the hardness of rocks to show how hard this rock is. What do I do when I compare? I need to add -er and -est to the adjective *hard* to help me make the comparison. I am going to use adjectives in my writing to help readers picture this unique rock. I could call the rock *long* and *sharp*, but instead, I describe it as *stretched* and *spiky*. I also know that I can select a word to emphasize with capitals or with boldface type. I am thinking I want to boldface the words *jagged shapes*, as that is so important to understanding this crystal.

> **Modeled Writing Sample**
>
> Dog Tooth Calcite
>
> Dog tooth calcite gets its unique name from its shape. Its shape is stretched and spiky, just like the teeth of dogs—only bigger! This crystal comes in a variety of dazzling colors, and they all have amazing jagged shapes. I wonder which crystal is the biggest of all?

TURN AND TALK Writers, what did I do to give readers a vivid picture of dog tooth calcite? What details help you picture this unique rock? Did I use the correct form of comparative adjectives? How can you tell which one to use?

CREATE AN AUTHENTIC PURPOSE Have students work individually or with partners to create reports about something they are studying in science, social studies, or a hobby or personal interest. Encourage them to include comparative and superlative adjectives and possessive pronouns if possible. Students should also include vivid adjectives that create clear pictures in readers' minds.

ASSESS THE LEARNING

- Gather the reports and see if your students are using vivid adjectives and comparative forms as well as possessive pronouns.
- Confer with writers about adjectives and comparative forms they have included in their writing to assess their understanding.

SUM IT UP Sometimes we think that report writing might be a little "dry" or boring, but it doesn't have to be boring at all! A science report about a rock can include exciting adjectives, comparisons that help readers get a clear picture, and even possessive pronouns. I am looking forward to displaying these reports so everyone can read them.

DAY 2 | Guided Practice

MODEL: HOW TO TRANSFER LEARNING TO ANOTHER CONTEXT Read to your students from Seymour Simon's *The Heart* or Stephen Kramer's *Caves* or another high-quality nonfiction selection. Think aloud as you identify powerful adjectives, comparative/superlative forms, or possessive pronouns from these books. Show your students how these authors replace tired, overused adjectives with livelier ones that help a reader to construct strong sensory images.

 TURN AND TALK Writers, these mentor books are amazing. What did you learn about comparatives, superlatives, adjectives, or possessive pronouns that you can apply to your own writing? Think together.

 CREATE AN AUTHENTIC PURPOSE Have partners review their writing folders together to find informational passages. Have them work together inserting powerful adjectives, including comparatives and superlatives. Have partners also search for possessive pronouns and mark them with sticky notes. Discuss their findings with partners and then debrief the whole group.

 ASSESS THE LEARNING

- As students reread their writing, note which students are still having difficulty using comparative and superlative adjectives and possessive pronouns.
- Gather small groups of readers to examine books by Seymour Simon and Stephen Kramer. Guide a conversation about adjective selection, including comparative and superlative forms.

SUM IT UP Writers, your eyes are getting sharper and your ears are getting better at hearing great descriptions with vivid adjectives. When you compare, you remember to think about whether you are comparing just two things or more than two, and you use the correct adjective form to compare. You should be proud of using these tools in your writing!

DAY 3 | Support and Extend the Learning

Select experiences that will best support your learners:

- Send students on an "adjective hunt." As students read independently or in small groups, have them place sticky notes near any adjectives that they think really pack a punch and create vivid pictures. After reading, students can contribute their ideas to a class list of powerful adjectives.

- Place a passage from a social studies, math, or science text on chart paper or a transparency. Ask students to suggest places where powerful adjectives could make the text more interesting and engaging for them. How do adjectives help nonfiction writing?

- Read a piece of nonfiction that includes powerful descriptions. Ask students to use those ideas in nonfiction writing of their own, then have partners share their rough drafts and highlight descriptions.

- Give students phrases to turn into possessives, focusing on content area writing. Phrases could include, for example, *the leaves of the flower*, *the grains of the crystal*, *the sum of the equation*, and so on (*the flower's leaves, the crystal's grains, the equation's sum*)

Pulling It All Together Cycle #12: Then and Now Books

Verbs: Present and Past Tenses • Verbs: Linking and Helping • Adverbs and Adverb Phrases as Sentence Openers

DAY 1 Model Writing for an Audience

Today, I am going to write some comparisons between schools today and schools long ago. This will be the beginning of a class book to celebrate our learning about life in the past. For things that happened long ago, I will use verbs in the past tense. For things today, I will use present tense. My first sentences are, *Today, some students can walk to school. Long ago, they all walked.* See the difference between the verbs? *Walk* is a verb that tells something that happens now, and *walk<u>ed</u>* tells about the past. I also used the word *can* in the first sentence. *Can* is a helping verb. It helps the verb *walk*. I am going to write another comparison, *Today, students type on a computer. Long ago, students wrote on personal chalkboards. . . .* I can make these sentences better with some adverbs. I am going to add *quickly* before *type*. That is an adverb that tells how they type. Help me think about how I might add an adverb to the last sentence to work with its verb (suggestions: *slowly, carefully*).

> ### Modeled Writing Sample
>
> Today, some students can walk to school. Long ago, they all walked. Today, students type on a computer. Long ago, students wrote on personal chalkboards or with quill pens and ink.

TURN AND TALK Writers, how did my verbs help to show the difference between long ago and today? How did the verb change? How many linking verbs or helping verbs did you notice? I really like the last sentence with the adverb phrase. What did you think of the way I changed that sentence?

CREATE AN AUTHENTIC PURPOSE Have students begin writing contributions to a "Then and Now" book. If they do not have knowledge of life in the past, consider having them compare and contrast themselves now and in kindergarten. Remind them to use verbs that signal the past and the present and to think about using helping verbs, linking verbs, and adverbs.

ASSESS THE LEARNING

- As students work, note on your Class Record-Keeping Grid (page 170) which students might need additional assistance in using the correct verb tense, linking and helping verbs, and adverbs and adverb phrases.

- During writing conferences, challenge students to insert adverbs into their writing to get a sense of their understanding.

SUM IT UP You also know a whole lot about verbs—tenses, helping verbs, linking verbs—and the adverbs that we can use to tell more about them, the when, where, how, and to what degree.

DAY 2 | Guided Practice

MODEL: HOW TO TRANSFER LEARNING TO ANOTHER CONTEXT Revisit a piece of modeled writing, looking carefully at the verbs. Model "testing" whether or not you have used the correct tense. Say: *This happened long ago, so I should use the past tense. I better change* talk *to* talked. *Consider places where you might use an adverb to tell more about the verb.*

 TURN AND TALK Writers, what did you notice about the adverbs I added? How did they help the verbs do a better job of telling about the action? What details do adverbs add to our sentences (*where, when, how,* and *to what degree*)? What is the difference between past-tense and present-tense verbs? How did I make sure I was using the correct one?

 CREATE AN AUTHENTIC PURPOSE Invite students to reread pieces from their own writing folders. Challenge them to identify places in which a verb could use some "beefing up" to be more descriptive and interesting. They can add helping verbs and/or adverb phrases to these verbs or choose a more specific verb, such as changing *quickly ran* to *dashed*.

 ASSESS THE LEARNING

- As students reread their writing, use your class record-keeping grid to track the use of mechanics in this cycle.
- In small-group instruction, have students identify present- and past-tense verbs, linking and helping verbs, and adverbs in their reading selections.

SUM IT UP Writers, I know you understand that mechanics can make your writing easier to read and much more interesting for your readers. You noticed that an adverb can help a verb. You know how to use linking and helping verbs in your writing, and you are remembering to add *-ed* to show that things happened in the past.

DAY 3 | Support and Extend the Learning

Select experiences that will best support your learners:

- Students may have difficulty remembering the linking and helping verbs. As students find examples of these in classroom texts, have them write the sentences in which they appear on sentence strips and add them to a class bulletin board for reference, or create resource lists for the walls featuring each of these verb types.

- *Slowly, quickly, lazily. . .* have students suggest adverbs that make writing more descriptive. Survey favorite literature for terrific adverbs and adverb phrases. Copy them onto strips and post on the walls.

- Another adverb activity students might enjoy is to make a card with an adverb on it, and then read a sentence in the way the card describes. They could read slowly, quickly, lazily, and so on.

PART IV

Tools

The tools presented in this section are designed to be time savers to support you and your students in creating a selection of resources that empower your work as writers.

The Teacher Resource: High-Frequency Writing Words on page 147 is an especially important resource from which you can draw words for spelling instruction, words for your word walls, and so on. These are the words most commonly used in writing, the words students need most! Use this list to power up your thinking and help you teach with maximum efficiency.

Take special note of the Create Your Own Resource pages. These are designed to support your students in creating a reference they can save and use over the course of the entire year. With sample sentences from mentor books and exemplars they create themselves, learners will have tools that will support and lift the writing they produce.

Contents

To print out the reproducibles on the following pages at full size, please visit: www.scholastic.com/masteringthemechanics.

Teacher Resource: High-Frequency Writing Words

This list of words represents those most commonly used in writing. Please note that word #1, *the*, occurs with the highest level of frequency while word #210, *took*, is the least commonly occurring in this high use group of words. Use this list to power up your word walls!

1 the	31 but	61 into	91 long	121 another	151 every	181 few
2 of	32 what	62 has	92 little	122 came	152 found	182 those
3 and	33 all	63 more	93 very	123 come	153 still	183 always
4 a	34 were	64 her	94 after	124 work	154 between	184 show
5 to	35 when	65 two	95 words	125 three	155 name	185 large
6 in	36 we	66 like	96 called	126 must	156 should	186 often
7 is	37 there	67 him	97 just	127 because	157 home	187 together
8 you	38 can	68 see	98 where	128 does	158 big	188 asked
9 that	39 an	69 time	99 most	129 part	159 give	189 house
10 it	40 your	70 could	100 know	130 even	160 air	190 don't
11 he	41 which	71 no	101 get	131 place	161 line	191 world
12 for	42 their	72 make	102 through	132 well	162 set	192 going
13 was	43 said	73 than	103 back	133 such	163 own	193 want
14 on	44 if	74 first	104 much	134 here	164 under	194 school
15 are	45 do	75 been	105 go	135 take	165 read	195 important
16 as	46 will	76 its	106 good	136 why	166 last	196 until
17 with	47 each	77 who	107 new	137 help	167 never	197 form
18 his	48 about	78 now	108 write	138 put	168 us	198 food
19 they	49 how	79 people	109 our	139 different	169 left	199 keep
20 at	50 up	80 my	110 me	140 away	170 end	200 children
21 be	51 out	81 made	111 man	141 again	171 along	201 feet
22 this	52 them	82 over	112 too	142 off	172 while	202 land
23 from	53 then	83 did	113 any	143 went	173 might	203 side
24 I	54 she	84 down	114 day	144 old	174 next	204 without
25 have	55 many	85 only	115 same	145 number	175 sound	205 boy
26 or	56 some	86 way	116 right	146 great	176 below	206 once
27 by	57 so	87 find	117 look	147 tell	177 saw	207 animal
28 one	58 these	88 use	118 think	148 men	178 something	208 life
29 had	59 would	89 may	119 also	149 say	179 thought	209 enough
30 not	60 other	90 water	120 around	150 small	180 both	210 took

From Rebecca Sitton's *Sourcebook for Teaching Spelling and Word Skills*, 2006, Egger Publishing, Inc. www.sittonspelling.com

Spelling Reference: Portable Word Wall

Name _____ * = Check Tricky Words Reference
(page 149)

A	D	H	K	O	S	U
a	dad	had	kids	of	said	under
about	day	happy	kitten	off	same	up
add	dear	has	know*	old	saw	us
after	did	have		on	say	use
again	do	he	**L**	once	school	
all	does	hear	let	one	see	**V**
an	down	help	like	only	set*	very
and		her	little	or	she	
any	**E**	here	live	other	should	**W**
are*	each	him	long	our*	so	want
as	even	his	look	own	some	was
at		home	looked		story	we
	F	how	love			were
B	family	hug		**P**	**T**	what
back	father		**M**	page	take	when*
be	find	**I**	mad	paper	tell	where
because	first	I	made	place	that	which
been	for*	if	make	play	the	who
big	friend	I'll	man	put	their*	why
boy	from	I'm	many	putting	them	would
but		in	me		then*	will
by*	**G**	into	men	**Q**	there*	with
	gave	is	mother	quiet	these	
C	get	it	much	**R**	they	**X**
called	girl	its*	must	ran	they're*	
came	give	it's*	my	read	this	**Y**
can	go			ready	to*	yes
city	going	**J**	**N**	really	today	you
come	good	jump	name	run		your*
could	got	just	new			you're*
			no*			
			not			**Z**
			now			

Spelling Reference: Tricky Words and Homophones

Belongs to _____ Date _____

Definition of homophones: Words that sound the same as another word
but have a different spelling and meaning.   *Homophones

Words	Examples
are * our * hour	Are you going to help? This is our house. The parade starts in one hour.
* buy * by * bye	Buy yourself a cool bike helmet. He walked right by me. The toddler waved, "Bye."
* for * four	Please go to the store for milk. Four is my favorite number.
* its * it's	The bike spun its tires. It's a gorgeous day!
* know * no	It's helpful to know your address. No, I don't want to go.
* lets * let's	Mom lets us drink juice. Let's go to the park!
set sit	Set the apple on the plate. Sit in the first seat.
than then	She is taller than you. Eat your lunch and then go to recess.
* their * there * they're	Their backyard is huge! Put the book over there. They're going to the library.
* to * too * two	They're going to the museum. I want to go, too! Did you eat way too much? We have two spotted puppies.
* your * you're	Your hair is a cool color! You're my best friend.
when win	When should we leave? Our team wants to win.

Create Your Own Resource: Using "ing" Words and Commas

Writer/Researcher _____ Date _____

Commas and "ing" words make terrific partners. They can help you create sentences that are creative, interesting, and filled with strong images for your reader. Adding action, images, and sounds to your sentences with "ing" words and commas makes them come alive!

Mentor sentences: "ing" phrases <u>followed</u> by a comma

<u>Dragging</u> his feet and <u>hanging</u> his head, Andrew slowly approached his furious mother.

<u>Barking</u> ferociously, the dog raced toward the cat.

You try it!

_____

_____

Find an "ing" phrase followed by a comma in a mentor book.

The sentence I found: _____

I found this in _____ (name of book) by

_____ on page _____.

Mentor sentence: Comma <u>before</u> "ing" phrases

Andrew slowly approached his furious mother, <u>dragging</u> his feet and <u>hanging</u> his head.

The dog raced toward the cat, <u>barking</u> ferociously.

You try it!

_____

_____

Find a comma before an "ing" phrase in a mentor book.

The sentence I found: _____

I found this in _____ (name of book) by

_____ on page _____.

© 2008 Hoyt & Therriault • Scholastic • *Mastering the Mechanics: Grades 2–3*

Create Your Own Resource: Combining Sentences With a Comma and a Linking Word

Writer/Researcher _____ Date _____

Commas and linking words can help us make short, choppy sentences into more interesting structures. These tools can help us create sentences that flow smoothly and sound more natural. Linking words often used include: *and*, *but*, *for*, *or*, *yet*, *so*.

Separate Sentences	Mentor Sentence
The dog barked. The cat raced toward the house.	The dog barked, <u>and</u> the cat raced toward the house.
I did my homework. I forgot it at home.	I did my homework, <u>but</u> I forgot it at home.

You try it!
Search mentor books to find a long sentence that is really two short sentences joined by a linking word and a comma.

The sentence I found: _____

I found this in _____ (name of book) on page _____. The linking

word is _____. If this had been written as two separate sentences, it might have looked like:

Sentence 1: _____

Sentence 2: _____

Find another one!
Search mentor books to find a long sentence that is really two short sentences joined by a linking word and a comma.

The sentence I found: _____

I found this in _____ (name of book) on page _____. The linking

word is _____. If this had been written as two separate sentences, it might have looked like:

Sentence 1: _____

Sentence 2: _____

What have you learned about creating longer, more natural sentences out of short sentences?

_____

_____

Create Your Own Resource: Transition Words

Writer/Researcher _____ Date _____

Transition words create connections between ideas and cue the reader about important information.

Transition words I found	They were located in (book)	The author's purpose in using them was to ….
_____	_____	_____
_____	_____	_____
_____	_____	_____
_____	_____	_____
_____	_____	_____

Purpose	Example of Transition Words
Time/sequence (the order in which something happens)	first, second, third, before, during, after, today, tomorrow, yesterday, until, next, then, as soon as, finally, afterward, earlier, meanwhile, now, since, soon
Show place	above, across, against, below, by, nearby, to the right of
Compare/contrast (show differences)	however, but, although, on the other hand, even though, still, though, yet, also, likewise
Conclude, summarize or emphasize a point (the end of the writing is coming)	finally, in conclusion, therefore, in other words
Add information	first, also, and, besides, in addition, for example, next, finally
Example or illustration	Specifically, for example, in fact, of course, to illustrate, for instance

Create Your Own Resource: Identifying Verb Types

Writer/Researcher _____ Date _____

Review your favorite books for examples of different kinds of verbs.

Action Verbs (These are the engines of sentences.)

_____ _____ _____ _____

Linking Verbs

_____ _____ _____ _____

Helping Verbs

_____ _____ _____ _____

My favorite mentor books for finding great verbs are: _____

A verb shows action or links the subject to another word in the sentence.

Action Verbs

An **action verb** tells what the subject is doing. Some experts think that verbs are the most important part of speech. They make writing specific and clear.

EXAMPLE: Ice cream *dribbled* down his chin. The worm *slithered* through the grass.

Linking Verbs

A **linking verb** links a subject to a noun or an adjective that comes after the verb.

EXAMPLE: My puppy *is* sweet.

Linking verbs: ("be" verbs) is, are, was, were, am, been

EXAMPLE: The painting *looks* strange. (Paintings don't see! *Looks* doesn't show action in this sentence. This sentence means the painting *is* strange.)

Other linking verbs: feel, look, remain, seem, smell, sound, taste (These words can be action words, too.)

Helping Verbs

Helping verbs come before the main verb and they help state the action or show when the action is taking place.

EXAMPLE: I *will* eat my breakfast. (The verb *will* helps tell about a future action, *will* eat.)

EXAMPLE: We *have been* waiting patiently. (The verbs *have been* help tell that an action is still happening, *have been* waiting.)

Helping Verbs: is, are, was, were, am, been, have, had, has, do, did, can, will, could, would, should, must, may, shall

When the verb is composed of two or more words, it is called a **verb phrase**.

Create Your Own Resource: Understanding Adverbs and Prepositional Phrases

Writer/Researcher _____ Date _____

Writers, grab a stack of your favorite books and start searching for adverbs and prepositional phrases. Notice how your favorite authors use prepositional phrases throughout their books. After you collect some great examples, challenge yourselves to liven up your writing with adverbs and prepositions that invite sensory imaging.

What did you notice about adverbs and prepositions in the books you reviewed? Which of the authors seemed to use them most? Write your favorite sentences that include adverbs or prepositional phrases below and tell where you found them.

_____ (sentence)

_____ (book)

_____ (sentence)

_____ (book)

_____ (sentence)

_____ (book)

Highlight the prepositions below that you found most often in the books you reviewed.

Adverbs tell where, when, why, and often end in "ly"
Slowly, quickly, sadly

Common Openers for Adverb Phrases
After, although, as, when, while, until, because, before, if, since

Common Prepositions
About, above, across, after, against, along, among, around, at, before, behind, below, beneath, beside, between, by, down, during, except, for, from, in, in front of, inside, instead of, into, like, near, of, off, on, on top of, out of, outside, over, since, through, to, toward, under, underneath, until, up, upon, with, within, without

---

See why writers simply ADORE THESE WORDS!

With grins on our faces, my friends and I stood at the edge of the pool. Without saying a word, we grabbed hands and blasted into the cool, crisp water. Around the edges, through the middle, and across the thrashing waves, we played like agile porpoises…

A challenge: Review your writing and find places where you can liven up sentences by beginning with a prepositional phrase!

© 2008 Hoyt & Therriault • Scholastic • *Mastering the Mechanics: Grades 2–3*

The Parts of Speech

Name _____ Grade _____

The English language has thousands of words, but each one can be placed in one of eight groups called the *parts of speech*.

Writers, after learning about each *part of speech*, include your own examples.

1. **Nouns:** name a person, place, thing, or idea (child, Carol, lake, honesty)

    _____

2. **Pronouns:** take the place of nouns (I, me, you, she, he, you, they, us)

    _____

3. **Verbs:** express action or state of being (skip, read, is, are)

    _____

4. **Adjectives:** describe a noun or a pronoun (awesome, fantastic, cool)

    _____

5. **Interjections:** express strong emotion or surprise (Whoa! Look out!)

    _____

6. **Connecting words:** connect words, groups of words, or sentences
    (and, or, because)

    _____

7. **Adverbs and adverb phrases:** tell where, how, and when; describe a verb,
    an adjective, or another adverb (on the roof, quickly, at high noon)

    _____

8. **Prepositions and prepositional phrases:** relate nouns or pronouns
    to another word in a sentence (on the steep roof, in the hidden box,
    under the low table, to the store)

    _____

Copy Editor's Symbols

Symbol	Meaning	Example
ϙ	Take it out.	I'm a g~~o~~ood writer.
∧	Put something in.	I'm a ^good^ writer.
∧#	Put in space.	I'm a∧good writer.
⊙	Add a period.	I'm a good writer⊙
≡	Make this a capital letter.	i'm a good writer.
/	Make this capital letter lowercase.	I'm a /Good writer.
sp	Spelling error.	I'm a good (writter.) sp

Used by permission from Ruth Culham's *6+1 Traits of Writing: Grades 3 and Up*

From the Desk of

_____

From the Desk of

_____

From the Desk of

_____

From the Desk of

_____

Interest Inventory

Name _____ Date _____

Date of birth _____ Number of siblings _____

Siblings' names _____

	Your favorite	Your least favorite
pet		
color		
food		
beverage		
restaurant		
subject		
book title		
author		
sport		
sports team		
theme park		
actor/athlete		
other		

Where have you lived?

City and state_____

Hobbies/interests: _____

List important qualities in a friend: _____

_____

Write whatever you would like to add: _____

_____

_____

Yearlong Planner

Consider: Are there any lessons that should appear multiple times?

	September	October	November	December	January	February	March	April	May	June
WEEK 1										
WEEK 2										
WEEK 3										
WEEK 4										

PART V

Assessment and Record Keeping

The assessment tools and record-keeping grids in this section are designed as suggestions. You may find that some match perfectly to the needs of your students or to your personal preferences in record keeping. We encourage you to make these tools your own or use them as springboards to create tools that are just right for you and your learners.

We have deliberately tried to highlight several kinds of tools for your consideration. You will notice that there are student self-reflections in the form of editing checklists, spelling self-reflections and "Skills I Can Use." There are cloze experiences to assess proficiency with pronouns and verbs. We encourage you to use these as models to create your own cloze experiences focused on any number of conventions and mechanics to support the development of your students. There are also several class record-keeping grids designed to support your observation of learners, create small groups with similar needs, and to assist you as you coach writers during individual conferences.

Most of all, select the tools that will empower you to watch your students closely. Observations and ongoing daily assessments give power to instruction, enabling you to respond to the needs of individuals, gather small groups with similar needs, or select from available resources. You are the driving force in instruction. You are the only one who truly understands your students' individual learning styles, and who can support their learning through targeted instruction.

To print out the reproducibles on the following pages at full size, please visit: www.scholastic.com/masteringthemechanics.

Contents

Editing Checklist I

Author _____ Peer Editor _____ Date _____

We have reviewed this work to check for:

Spelling   ❑

Capitalization

    Beginning of sentence   ❑

    Names   ❑

    Titles   ❑

Punctuation

    End of sentence (. ? !)   ❑

    Complete sentences   ❑

Editing Checklist I

Author _____ Peer Editor _____ Date _____

We have reviewed this work to check for:

Spelling   ❑

Capitalization

    Beginning of sentence   ❑

    Names   ❑

    Titles   ❑

Punctuation

    End of sentence (. ? !)   ❑

    Complete sentences   ❑

Editing Checklist II

Author _____ Peer Editor _____ Date _____

We have reviewed this work to check for:

SPELLING

❑ We corrected spelling on: _____, _____, _____.

❑ We checked the tricky word list, including homophones.

CAPITALIZATION

❑ Beginning of sentence

❑ Names and proper nouns (English muffin)

❑ Titles

❑ A word all in caps for emphasis

PUNCTUATION

❑ End of sentence (. ? !)

❑ Sentence opener followed by a comma

❑ Compound sentence joined by a linking word and a comma

COMPLETE SENTENCES

(Who/what did something? What did they do?)

❑ This piece is free of fragments.

SOME INTERESTING SENTENCES

The most interesting sentence in this piece is _____

_____

_____.

We think this sentence is strong because _____

_____

_____

© 2008 Hoyt & Therriault • Scholastic • *Mastering the Mechanics: Grades 2–3*

Editing Checklist III: Peer Editing

Author _____ Peer Editor _____ Date _____

We have reviewed this work to check for:

SPELLING

❏ Three words we corrected: _____, _____, _____.

❏ We checked the tricky word list, including homophones.

❏ We checked to be sure there was a vowel in every syllable.

❏ Resources we used to correct spelling include: _____.

CAPITALIZATION

❏ Beginning of sentence

❏ Names and proper nouns (English muffin)

❏ Titles

❏ A word all in caps for emphasis

PUNCTUATION

❏ End of sentence (. ? !)

❏ Apostrophe for possessive (Anna's bike)

❏ Sentence opener followed by a comma

❏ Compound sentence joined by a linking word and a comma

❏ Exclamation point for interjection

❏ Items in a series are separated by commas

SENTENCES

(Who/what did something? What did they do?)

❏ This piece is free of fragments.

❏ This piece has no run-on sentences. The word *and* is used with caution.

SOME INTERESTING SENTENCES

The most interesting sentence in this piece is _____

_____.

We think this sentence is strong because _____

_____.

© 2008 Hoyt & Therriault • Scholastic • *Mastering the Mechanics: Grades 2–3*

Editing Checklist IV: Focus on Grammar

Author _____ Peer Editor _____ Date _____

We have reviewed this work to check for:

VERBS

❏ Verb tense is consistent throughout (all past tense or all present tense).

❏ Verb case is correct: *We saw a plane* vs. *We seen a plane.*

❏ Verb endings: There is subject-verb agreement for singulars and plurals.

PRONOUNS

❏ The reader can clearly tell who a pronoun refers to (antecedent).

❏ Pronouns clearly show gender and number (he, she, they, we).

Word order and choice. Sentences are written in conventional form.

❏ There are no double subjects (My mom, she…).

❏ There are no double negatives (We don't got no…).

Our favorite sentence is _____.

We picked this because _____.

SOME INTERESTING SENTENCES

The most interesting sentence in this piece is _____

_____

We think this sentence is strong because _____

_____.

© 2008 Hoyt & Therriault • Scholastic • *Mastering the Mechanics: Grades 2–3*

Spelling Strategies Self-Assessment

Writer_____ Date _____

Mark the strategies you use: (Put a star next to the ones you use the most.)

❑ Stretch words out slowly and listen to sounds

❑ Draw a line under words I am not sure of during drafting or write *sp*

❑ Clap out the syllables and check each syllable for a vowel

❑ Try to visualize what the word looks like

❑ Use another piece of paper or the margin to spell the word several ways

❑ Use words I know to spell other words

❑ Use a portable word wall

❑ Use the class word wall

❑ Refer to the tricky words and homophone lists

❑ Use a dictionary

❑ Use a thesaurus

❑ If I know I can find the word quickly, I might _____.

❑ If I think it will take me some time to find the correct spelling, I wait until editing,
and then I might _____.

❑ During editing, ask a friend to edit with me

❑ During editing, add words to my portable word wall that I think I will use again

When I come to a word I am not sure of during drafting, I usually _____

or _____. During editing, I would follow up on the word

by checking _____ or _____.

If I were to give advice to a younger student about spelling, I would tell that writer:

_____

_____

Interactive Assessment

Focus on capitalization, spelling, punctuation, grammar, spacing, or editing.

Date _____ Title of Writing _____ Author_____

Dear Parent,

Thank you for joining our celebration of your student's writing. Please add your response and return this form and the writing to school tomorrow.

The Author

As I look at this writing and editing, I am especially proud of _____
_____
_____
_____
_____

Author _____

The Teacher

As I look at this writing and editing, I am especially proud of _____
_____
_____
_____
_____

Teacher _____

Through the Eyes of a Parent

As I look at this writing and editing, I am especially proud of _____
_____
_____
_____
_____

Parent _____

Skills I Can Use

Name _____

Skill used in my writing	I started using this on (date) _____

Assessment Tool: Cloze for Verb Tenses

Oops!

Scrape! Skid… Screetch! The skateboards _____ across the sidewalk and right into the door of the grocery store. Splat! Down _____ three laughing boys. As they _____ on the floor giggling hysterically, they realized they _____ right at the feet of the furious store owner.

"You crazy kids! I _____ you if you ever _____ your skateboards into my store again. I would _____ your parents," _____ the grocer.

"Stand still and don't _____. This is only the beginning of your troubles. Wait until your parents _____ what you have done." He _____ to the phone and started to dial.

skid	skidded	call	called
go	went	roar	roared
roll	rolled	move	moved
was	were	see	saw
tell	told	stomp	stomped
ride	rode		

© 2008 Hoyt & Therriault • Scholastic • *Mastering the Mechanics: Grades 2–3*

Note to teacher: Place this selection on the overhead or provide copies for partners.

Assessment Tool: Cloze for Pronoun Proficiency

News Bulletin: Dangerous Wolf Trashes Brick House
By Lynnette Brent and Linda Hoyt

_____ dispatcher sent me out on an emergency run. _____ had a story to write but _____ had to wait. _____ leaped into the news van and raced to the scene. There was this huge, shaggy wolf stomping around standing outside this brick house. _____ was yelling and making all kinds of noise. Man, this wolf was upset!

_____ yelled that the pig had said bad things about _____ granny. The wolf was huffing and puffing and looked like _____ was trying to blow the house down! Even though _____ knows you can't blow down a house made of bricks, it was pretty scary to watch. The spectators were getting so worked up watching, _____ started moving back away from the action.

This wolf had already eaten two pigs. _____ is definitely dangerous and _____ know _____ was not going near him. Before _____ had a chance to wolf down another ham dinner, I called 911 for the police so _____ could take _____ to jail and lock him up. Both the police and _____ are ready to call this one a wrap!

I
my
it
he
his
they
everyone
us
both
myself
these
those
nobody
him
we
they

Note to teacher: Place this selection on the overhead or provide copies for partners. Their task is to insert appropriate pronouns and identify the nouns (antecedents) to which they refer.

Class Record-Keeping Grid

Class Record-Keeping Grid: Capitalization

	Proper nouns: people	Proper nouns: places	Proper nouns: things	Titles used with names (President Lincoln)	Abbreviations	Titles of books, magazines	Days and months	First word of direct quotation

Class Record-Keeping Grid: Commas

	Items in a list	After a signal word at the beginning of sentence	To separate person talked to from rest of sentence	Sentence opener, then a comma	To separate clauses	To separate month and year in a date	In greeting and closing in a letter

Class Record-Keeping Grid: Rules of Dialogue	1) Place quotation marks around the exact words of the speaker.	2) Capitalize the first word of a direct quotation.	3) Include end punctuation marks, sometimes a comma, inside the quotation marks.	4) Identify the speaker.	*Use alternatives for the overused verb said.

Double Subjects

Name _____ Grade _____

Directions:
- Proofread these sentences looking for "double subject" errors.
- Edit sentences with a "doubling up" error by crossing out the error.

1. Kathy is an excellent swim coach.

2. Kathy, she is an excellent swim coach.

3. My kitty, she laps up milk with her cute little tongue. Slurp!

4. My kitty laps up milk with her cute little tongue. Slurp!

5. Mrs. Toad and Mrs. Frog, they are dear, dear friends.

6. Mrs. Toad and Mrs. Frog are dear, dear friends.

7. My sister loves to play soccer, baseball, and basketball!

8. My sister, she loves to play soccer, baseball, and basketball!

9. Running in circles, my dog, he raced around the room chasing his tail. It was hilarious!

10. Running in circles, my dog raced around the room chasing his tail. It was hilarious!

Write a sentence or two of your own for fun!

_____

_____

_____

_____

_____

© 2008 Hoyt & Therriault • Scholastic • *Mastering the Mechanics: Grades 2–3*

Note to teacher: These sentences are to stimulate discussion. Please display them on the overhead, or a chart, or provide copies of this page for partners. **Please do not ask students to recopy these sentences.**

Pronoun Order and Use

Name _____ Grade _____

Directions:
- Proofread sentences looking for:
  - proper order of nouns and pronouns
  - proper pronoun use
- Edit sentences by crossing out the error and writing the correct word or words.
- Do NOT recopy the sentences!

1. Kim and I wore the exact same dress!

2. Sometimes me and my brother fight like cats and dogs.

3. My puppy and I both slept late!

4. Linda and me asked different math questions.

5. Me and Bob played our favorite baseball game in the vacant lot.

6. Did the principal and I just laugh at that joke?

7. I and my cousin love to play soccer!

8. My friends and I went for a long, relaxing walk.

9. Me and my friends went for a long, relaxing walk.

10. I and Mary talked on the phone for an hour!

© 2008 Hoyt & Therriault • Scholastic • *Mastering the Mechanics: Grades 2–3*

Note to teacher: These sentences are to stimulate discussion. Please display them on the overhead, or a chart, or provide copies of this page for partners. **Please do not ask students to recopy these sentences.**

To print out these reproducibles at full size, please visit www.scholastic.com/masteringthemechanics.

My fat Tail Lepord Casey
Geko has a fat tail.
I hold hime every day.
Some times he climes
on my bed. his name
is Jake. hise favorit
thing to eat is meal
worms. He lives in a
ten golen fish tanck.
He has a lot of
room. hise favorit things to do are
eat slepe a stae still.

Febuary 2nd

Dear Aunt, Niva,

Guess what I got for my bithday? Give up?
A dog!! I love my dog. she looKs like
a dog that was Patid blaK. she sounds
liK a cat wen she barKs. she is so blak she's
siny. she lisens to me. sometimes we let
her go to my gradmas haus And let her PlaY
whith bud. I drew You a picher to.

Love and Hugs. Saro
and
Kissus ooo
xx

P.S. write bak soon!

Interest Inventory

Name: Michelle P.

Date: (day, month, date, year) Monday September 8, 2005
DOB: October 27, 1997
# of siblings: 2
Siblings' names: Mary Matt

Your favorite: Your least favorite:
- food: pizza   eggplant
- beverage: milk   black coffee
- restaurant: red robin   ?
- subject: math AND reading and writing) ?
- book title: The bravest dog ever Balto
- author: JK Rowling   ?
- sport: baseball   basket ball
- sports team: Atlanta Braves
- theme park: Disneyland   ?
- actor/athlete:

Where have you lived?
- city and state Modesto california
  Seattle washington Denver colorado

Hobbies/interests: American Girl Dolls, postcards
Salt and pepper shakers
Write whatever you would like to add:

My favorite teacher is my kindergarten
Mrs. Murphy.

My favorite letter Mm ☺
I like to write my name in cursive. See Michelle P.
My sister taught me.

Bus Rides
by J. D.

I ride on a skool bus just like every body els. It seems to take for ever. I hav to get up by 6:30 to cach the bus by 7. Win its rainy and cold, the frist bus step can be xtreemly slippery. Since my little sister and me are the frist on the bus we get to sit on the bak seat. Its like a xtra long bench. She sits by one windo and I sit by the other. We look out the windo and wach cars zip by. Then we do the same thing on the way home. Its sort ov boring but its better then waking.

I ride on a **skool** bus just like every body <u>els</u>. It seems to take for ever. **I hav** to get up by 6:30 to *cach* the bus by 7. **Win** its rainy and cold, the **frist** bus step can be <u>xtreemly</u> slippery. Since my little sister and me are the frist on the bus we get to sit on the back seat. Its like a <u>xtra</u> long bench. She sits by one <u>windo</u> and I sit by the other. We look out waching the cars zip by. Then we do the same thing on the way home. Its sort ov boring but its better then *waking*.

Bus Rides • © 2008 Hoyt & Therriault • Scholastic • *Mastering the Mechanics: Grades 2–3*

Note:
- **Bolded words** are on the portable word wall, page 148 (**school**, **when**, **first**, **of**)
- <u>Underlined words</u> would probably remain "sounding out" words unless the piece was to be published. Then the teacher would act as editor to correct remaining spelling errors.
- *Italicized words* could be added to J. D.'s personal word wall (*catch*, *walk*)

The Perfect Day
By Darrel T.

Yesterday was a great day. It was snowing and snowing. It lasted all night and school was cancelled so my best friend and I built things in the snow ALL day long. There were snow people with faces and sticks for arms. They looked like marshmallow people. One time, we looked up and saw that the head had fallen off our snow boy. It rolled off and had landed with a big splat! We laughed and LAUGHED until we made strange noises with our noses. That made us laugh even More. My dog started barking and made a GRRRRR sound when we put the coats and hats on the snow people. He is pretty dumb sometimes. That made us start laughing all over again. Yesterday was a PERFECT day!

The Perfect Day • © 2008 Hoyt & Therriault • Scholastic • *Mastering the Mechanics: Grades 2–3*

June 4th

The best day of the year is when I get to see my grandma and grandpa. They are always excited to see ME! They live way far away in Peru. It takes us forever! First there is the plane. Then there is a bus full of peple on bumpy roads. Forever!! Forever!! Forever!! But it is all werth it because they love ME! I love them so! ~~much~~ Dont you LOVE Grandparents?

How An Octopus Protects Herself

An octopus has many ways to protect herself. First, She can take her eight legs and wrap them around other animals. She can use the suction cups on her legs to grip things. When an animals tries to attack her, she can make her body squish together so she can hide out in little places. That was a surprise to me! An octopus can squirt ink into the water and blind the attacker for a little bit of time. Then she swims off. Pretty cool. ~~ways~~ ~~to protect herself~~

by Stephanie J.

How an Octopus Protects Herself • © 2008 Hoyt & Therriault • Scholastic • Mastering the Mechanics: Grades 2–3

A Cricket's Five Senses

Written by George M.

Part 1: "A Cricket's Eyes"

The cricket has five senses but there are distinct differences. While we have only two eyes a cricket has five. Some of the crickets eyes let him see dark and light and some of his eyes let him see in a lot of places at one time. If you think a crickets eyes are cool wait until you hear about the crickets ears.

Part 2: "A Cricket's Ears"

A crickets ears are not where you would expect, they are on his legs! A cricket can stretch out its legs and "hear" all kinds of noises that a persons ear couldn't pick up.

A Cricket's Five Senses • © 2008 Hoyt & Therriault • Scholastic • *Mastering the Mechanics: Grades 2–3*

Dear Mrs. Hoyt,

Thank you for everything. I loved the way you did things also I liked the web of undurstanding it was cool. I had fun with everything. I hope you have a good trip Home to oregon.

Love,
Kala

Read books.

June 3, 2007

Dear new 2nd grader,

You're going to like 2nd grade. I just KNOW it! Here are some of the cool things you didn't get to do in 1st grade. but you get to do now. You'll be able to eat your snack DURING writing, keep your water bottle on your desk and have five more minutes for lunch. Then you get to stay in the recess line until the 1st graders go in. In 2nd grade you get to do cool science experiments have pe 3 days a week instead of 2 and get to help with the k class. Be sure to bring your pencils, paper erasers and box of Kleenex by Friday. If everybody brings everything Mrs. M will give you a cool treat.

Your friend,

Zane P.

Me and My Cousin

by Martha P.

Me and my cousins are very close. We even live on the same block and see each other every day. My favorite cousin is Jordon. She and me like to do a lot of the same things. We both like to make cookies. The whole house smells SO good. Her favorite cookie is chocolate chip. So is mine. Her favorite ice cream is chocolate-chocolate chip. So is mine. Her favorite candy is Hershey's chocolate bar, but I like M & M's. Oh, well. Two out of three is a lot in common!

A walrus went swiming
in the Ocean one day
he jumt in the water
and all fish swan away
his tusks were sharp
and long and white.
they no he can eat
them all in
one bite.

Bird Watching Field Trip

Last weekend my family we went bird watching. I thought it was going to be boring and didn't want to go. My parents they told me that we were going as a family and we were going to have fun whether I liked it or not. They smiled at me and I frowned at them. To make a long story short we had an ok time. We saw hawks, swallows, and some really cool flicker. I used binoculars for the first time, got to walk across a stream on slippery rocks, and got ice cream on the way home. I guess sometimes parents they make good plans.

Racoon

While we sleep, he trundles on light feet confident and sure. Quietly, his shadow moves through the darkness, searching. Within the misty night, his masked face and glowing eyes keep careful watch for predator and prey. Shhh! He pauses. _____

_____

"Birds Eat"
by Tommy T.

Seeds. Fruit. Insects. Birds eat all of these foods. Parrots use powerful beaks to crack open nuts and seeds. A toucan's giant, colorful bill picks fruits and berries from tree branches. Almost all birds eat insects, but woodpeckers <u>really</u> know how to catch bugs. They use a long tongue to pull bugs from underneath the bark on trees. Gross, cool too!

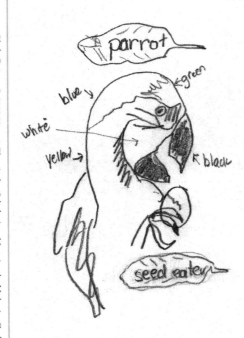

the dark

Some people fear the dark

Darkness has the power to make you feel alone. Without light, your imagination can make you think that harmless things are suddenly scary.

Things are different for nocturnal animals.

Nocturnal animals love the dark because they can see very well. Their eyes are especially large and can reflect even small amounts of light back into the eye.

The Dark • © 2008 Hoyt & Therriault • Scholastic • Mastering the Mechanics: Grades 2–3

Head Lice

I have this teacher She is really nice. But some time I think She has head lice. She itches all day. And the last time for head lice check She got sent home from school. I would tell you more but it is not cool. The day she came back She had no hair and her head was bear. I think to my self how did she get the lice. I kept on thinking untell I new that I was not nice because I'm the one who gave her the lice.

By: Samantha

Head Lice • © 2008 Hoyt & Therriault • Scholastic • Mastering the Mechanics: Grades 2–3

The Legends class included many bona fide legends. Though it was open to any rider who had previously raced the event. Malcolm Smith (1) was literally mobbed at the starting line for autographs and photos. He and Ty Davis's dad, Terry, were the fastest of the Legends riders over 50 years old. Davis finished and MS was in 1th P...

Team Kawasaki's Jeff Emig is the only person painted in McGrath's path. It took a perfect season. If an for his perennial archrival taking three wins in the first six months of the season, McGrath might have had a 22-race winning streak going!

Facemask

Gloves

Boots

Shirt Helmet

Chestguard

Pants

Finish

BIBLIOGRAPHY

Anderson, J. (2005). *Mechanically inclined: Building grammar, usage, and style into writer's workshop.* Portland, ME: Stenhouse.

Angelillo, J. (2002). *A fresh approach to teaching punctuation: Helping young writers use conventions with precision and purpose.* New York: Scholastic.

Calkins, L. & Louis, N. (2003). *Writing for readers: Teaching skills and strategies.* Portsmouth, NH: Heinemann.

Culham, R. (2003). *6+1 traits of writing: The complete guide: Grades 3 and up.* New York: Scholastic.

Department of Education, Western Australia. (2006). *Writing map of development* (2nd ed.).

Fletcher, R. & Portalupi, J. (2001). *Writing workshop: The essential guide.* Portsmouth, NH: Heinemann.

Graves, D. (1994). *A fresh look at writing.* Portsmouth, NH: Heinemann.

Harwayne, S. (2001). *Writing through childhood: Rethinking process and product.* Portsmouth, NH: Heinemann.

Harwayne, S. (1992). *Lasting impressions: Weaving literature into the writing workshop.* Portsmouth, NH: Heinemann.

Ray, K. W. (1999). *Wonderous words.* Portsmouth, NH: Heinemann.

Ray, K. W. & Cleaveland, L. (2004). *About the authors: Writing workshop with our youngest writers.* Portsmouth, NH: Heinemann.

Routman, R. (2004). *Writing essentials: Raising expectations and results while simplifying teaching.* Portsmouth, NH: Heinemann.

Sitton, R. (2006). *Rebecca Sitton's sourcebook for teaching spelling and word skills.* Scottsdale, AZ: Egger Publishing, Inc.

Taylor, B. M., Pearson, P. D., Peterson, D. S., & Rodriguez, M. C. (2002). Looking inside classrooms: Reflecting on the "how" as well as the "what" in effective reading instruction. *The Reading Teacher, 56* (3), 270–279.

Topping, D. H. & Hoffman, S. J. (2006). Getting grammar: 150 new ways to teach an old subject. Portsmouth, NH: Heinemann.

INDEX